CW00545749

The Colours of West Yorkshire

Don Akrigg

Capital Transport

Acknowledgements

First and foremost my thanks are to the dedicated photographers who took colour images when film was expensive and not always easy to obtain. I have tried to ensure that each image is correctly attributed to its photographer – my apologies to anyone whose picture is wrongly named.

Of equal importance have been the weeks of dedicated work by the writing team:

David Allen (West Riding, Bullock, South Yorkshire Motors)

Peter Cardno (Hanson, Huddersfield, Baddeley, County)

Ted Gadsby (West Yorkshire Road Car)

Tony Hall (the smaller independents)

John Kaye (Leeds, Ledgard)

Mike Russell (trolleybuses)

Peter Waller (Bradford).

John Stringer, John Kaye and Peter Greaves read the text and checked innumerable details. Tony Hall convinced me the project was well worth doing – and kept on doing so. In addition to his usual painstaking work on the images, Mike Eyre ensured our work aligned with the style of the Colours Series.

The definitive books by Jim Soper (Leeds), Peter Cardno (Huddersfield), Stanley King (Bradford), Geoffrey Hilditch (Halifax), Ralph Wilkinson (Todmorden), Don Bate (Ledgard) and Robin Hannay (Guy Wulfrunian) have been invaluable sources as have the archives of the Omnibus Society and the publications of the PSV Circle.

I hope therefore that there are few mistakes; inevitably there will be some – and they are mine.

Enjoy the book. There are some splendid images – hopefully at least one is of your favourite vehicle or place.

Don Akrigg

Front cover Many routes in the west of the county involved steep climbs to reach villages perched high on the edge of the Pennines. Set against a background of the houses and mills of West Vale, Greetland, Halifax Joint Omnibus Committee's Metro-Cammell-bodied AEC Regent V 216, new in 1960, tackles the long climb from West Vale towards Stainland bound for Outlane. *Linden Edwards*

Back cover New in 1947 West Yorkshire Road Car 208 (later SG103) was later rebuilt for one-man operation, re-entering service in February 1956; it ran until 1962. The conversion was somewhat unusual. The bulkhead was partially removed, the driver had a swivel chair and his access was from the saloon – notice there was no cab door handle; also the absence of opening windows – ventilation was by air ducts. Seating capacity was reduced from 35 to 30; the rear door was unaltered but permanently locked. After a short trial in Harrogate, it was one of the four 'cars' (as West Yorkshire called its buses) allocated to Grassington depot. The grey spot by its fleet number indicates its 'home' depot – Keighley. The background to this picture of SG103 is the fifteenth century Barden Tower. Service 75 from Grassington to Ilkley was one of the most picturesque bus journeys in Britain, following the winding River Wharfe along the dale, through Burnsall, Appletreewick, Bolton Abbey and Addingham. In 1959 the single fare for the 70-minute run was 2s 1d. It was a gem of a journey on an immaculate bus. *Geoffrey Morant* 1959

Frontispiece Come rain or sunshine, Bradford's attractive blue and cream livery was a cheerful sight and the purchase of good used trolleybuses was a clever and cost-effective way of prolonging the life of its trolleybus network. Passing Carr Lane in Windhill on its way to Shipley and Saltaire, working the circuitous route 40 from Forster Square, is one of the eight 1950 BUT trolleybuses acquired from St Helens in 1958. Unlike most other second-hand purchases, these vehicles were not rebodied but retained their original 56-seat East Lancs bodywork, extensively renovated. This view dates from 22 June 1971 – the route was converted to motorbus operation from 1 July. Fleet number 795 was the second BUT 9611T to be built; originally St Helens 183 (later 383) it was withdrawn on this conversion. *Michael Russell*

First published 2013

ISBN 978-1-85414-370-9

Published by Capital Transport Publishing Ltd
www.capitaltransport.com

Printed by 1010 Printing International Ltd

© Capital Transport Publishing 2013

Images copyright of the photographers as named

Contents

Introduction   4
Bradford   6
County Motors   22
Halifax   28
Hanson   46
Hebble   52
Huddersfield   58
Ledgard   72
Leeds   82
Todmorden   100
West Riding (including Bullock & Sons)   106
West Yorkshire   124
Yorkshire Woollen   134
The Independents   142

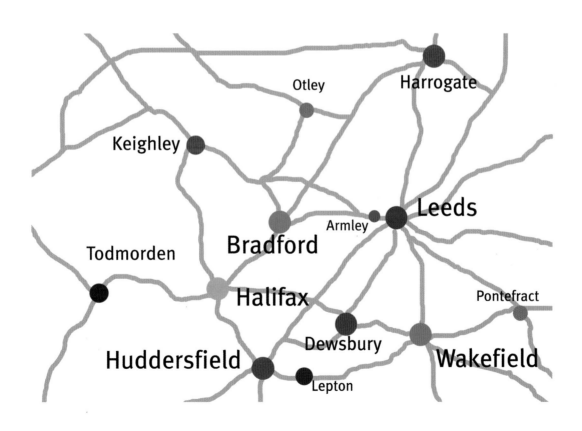

Introduction

For centuries, the White Rose County of Yorkshire was divided into three 'ridings' – North Riding, East Riding and West Riding. Local government reorganisation on 1st April 1974 replaced the Ridings with the Metropolitan counties of North Yorkshire, South Yorkshire, West Yorkshire and Humberside.

Although the cut-off date for this book is the formation of those Metropolitan Counties, practicality made it convenient that the area it covers is the Metropolitan county of West Yorkshire, adding a small part of North Yorkshire so as to include Pennine Motor Services and the Harrogate-based West Yorkshire Road Car Company.

The geography of the area includes cities, large towns and small towns, all heavily industrialised; ribbon-development along deep Pennine valleys, high moorlands and villages and last but by no means least, the grandeur of the Yorkshire Dales. Combined with this mix of industrial, moorland and rural landscapes, the area's public transport system was not only one of the most interesting but also the probably most photogenic in the country.

The West Riding's principal industries – textiles, chemicals, engineering and coal mining – were labour intensive. Thus there were rich pickings for operators of public transport service in the many industrial areas, with thousands of workers needing to travel to and from work. The result was a very wide variety of road transport operators. First were the municipalities, keen to serve beyond their boundaries, and the railways and large groups, keen to claim territory within and beyond municipal boundaries. Thus the area was unique in having three municipal operators which formed Joint Committees with the railways – Halifax, Huddersfield and Todmorden. By contrast, being much larger, Leeds and Bradford avoided this. The large 'group' companies were Yorkshire Woollen and Hebble – members of the BET group – and one Tilling company – West Yorkshire, which itself had joint subsidiaries which ran the buses in York and Keighley on behalf of the local authority.

Then there were the independents not associated with any group. Until its sale to the Transport Holding Company in 1968, West Riding was the largest independent operator in the country. Farsley Omnibus and Kippax Motors became part of the mighty Wallace Arnold coaching organisation. Samuel Ledgard was a legend in his own right; Ezra Layock started running buses in 1905. The Simpson family have run Pennine for almost a century; Lord Hanson is a famous name in 21st century business; South Yorkshire grew from a feud in the Bullock family; Phyllis Bingley was known by fellow operators as 'formidable'. Baddeley Brothers, Ford, Wood, Longstaff, Everett and Cooper Brothers were equally distinctive. Led by determined families they fiercely guarded their businesses against the big operators. Several outlived the major companies, the formation of the Passenger Transport Executive and industry deregulation in 1986. It would be wrong to refer to any of them as 'small'.

The Leeds tramway system outlasted those of Bradford, Halifax, Huddersfield, Dewsbury, Wakefield and Keighley; it has been covered in a companion volume in this series of books. The area was early into trolleybus systems and Bradford and Huddersfield built extensive systems. Huddersfield's ran until 1968 and the Bradford system, which closed in March 1972, was the final trolleybus system of its type in the country.

Leeds was home to the well known coachbuilder Charles H Roe Ltd whose works were at Crossgates in the eastern suburbs. The firm's high quality bodies were the first choice for most of the operators in Yorkshire and beyond – typified by Leeds' AEC Regent V 951. Leeds had a comprehensive destination display until 1962 when a new layout was introduced removing the intermediate points to leave just the route number and final destination as on the front and rear of the buses in this March 1967 view outside the large Central Bus Station. *Geoffrey Morant*

Samuel Ledgard was a legendary figure far beyond the bus industry – he was licensee of the Nelson Hotel at Armley for over 50 years. Death duties caused problems for his executors in running the business and from that point on large numbers of second hand vehicles were purchased including many AECs from London Transport most were highbridge, there being only four lowbridge examples as the Weymann-bodied one seen here in August 1967 with the Horsforth War Memorial as a backdrop. *Alan Mortimer*

The happier days of West Riding before the Wulfrunian are captured in this June 1968 picture of Roe-bodied AEC Reliance 925 in the country town of Selby. Roe bodies dominated the West Riding fleet and although the double-deckers were mainly Leylands and Guys, AECs were favoured for a large part of the single-deck fleet. *Geoffrey Morant*

There was variety in the chassis and bodies of the various fleets' trolleybuses and buses. Although there were plenty of Leylands, Guys and Daimlers, the area was something of an AEC stronghold, in contrast to the other side of the Pennines where Leyland ruled. Not unexpectedly, the majority of bodywork came from the famous Crossgates Carriage Works, Leeds, of Charles H Roe Ltd and this was not just a matter of local support for, as many have commented, 'Roe never built a bad body'. The area was also notable for more rebodying than usual, in particular of single-deckers into double-deckers.

Less happy was the West Riding company's involvement with the Guy Wulfrunian, where the firm seemed to forget its main task was running buses and instead became involved in design and development of the model, rushing into buying a large fleet which proved so troublesome that it brought the company to financial ruin. It was then bought by the nationalised Transport Holding Company ('THC') and in 1969 along with the THC's other bus interest, passed to the National Bus Company ('NBC'). The story is covered elsewhere but there is extra coverage of the Wulfrunian in the book.

All this created an unrivalled kaleidoscope of colours – until the 1970s. West Riding had passed to NBC, Todmorden merged with Halifax, Hebble and County were broken up, Hanson's bus fleet was sold to Huddersfield. The NBC then introduced its standard liveries of poppy red or leaf green, which few could call attractive. More colour vanished in 1974 with the creation of the West Yorkshire Passenger Transport Executive, with its head office at Wakefield. It took over the municipal fleets and went on to acquire the Baddeley Brothers and the United Services businesses and also Hanson's coach company.

The book therefore ends with the formation of the PTE but it is perhaps appropriate to mention that the PTE adopted the fleetname Metro and (after some local variation trials) a Verona green and buttermilk livery – and that some of the National Bus Company's vehicles were also painted into the PTE livery.

This is not a history book – the history of each operator is well covered elsewhere. It is a collection of fine colour pictures of the area's buses and trolleybus at work, taken in the 1950s, 1960s and early 1970s by first-rate photographers.

This picture illustrates the changes in the company fleets that took place at the end of the 1960s. Hebble's final single-deck service buses were two AEC Reliances with Marshall bodywork, delivered in 1969. When Hebble ceased operating stage services in February 1971 they passed to Yorkshire Woollen District and 275 is pictured in summer 1972 loading in Broad Street, Halifax, on the direct route to Leeds. The vehicle in the background is Calderdale JOC 359, one of three Leyland Leopards acquired from Yorkshire Traction. *Linden Edwards*

Bradford

The second largest of the municipal fleets to pass to West Yorkshire PTE on 1 April 1974, Bradford City Transport possessed a fleet of some 315 double-deck and 12 single-deck buses at this date. However, it is as an operator of trolleybuses that Bradford will always have a place in transport history.

It was in June 1911 that Bradford, along with neighbouring Leeds, introduced this form of transport to public service in Britain; whilst Leeds was to abandon the trolleybus in 1928, the trackless continued to give sterling service to Bradford until final withdrawal in March 1972 — a 61-year period unmatched by any other trolleybus operator in the country.

Municipal operation of public transport in Bradford started with the first 4ft 0in electric tramcars in 1898. The pre-existing horse and steam tramways were taken over in 1902. The tramway network was to expand, with the last extension being opened in October 1914.

Following the first short route – from Dudley Hill to Laisterdyke – the trolleybus network was to grow, with extensions to the original route to Bolton and Bankfoot, and new routes to Bolton Woods, Frizinghall, Oakenshaw and Clayton. It was not until 1929, however, with the conversion of the Allerton trams route to trolleybus operation that the city's tramway network started significantly to contract.

By that date, a third form of transport – the motorbus – had appeared with the introduction, in 1926, of a batch of AEC 413s. The new arrivals were designed to extend the Corporation's areas of operation as well as compete with local operators in an era before the Road Transport Act of 1930 introduced regulated services.

Over the next decade, the tramway network shrank; if it had not been for the outbreak of war trams would have disappeared much earlier than May 1950. The war, however, was to have another long-lasting impact upon the fleet – the loan of Southend-on-Sea trolleybuses resulted in the decision to replace the existing Prussian Blue livery with a much lighter shade

In the post war years it seemed likely that the trolleybuses would soon follow the tram into oblivion. However, the appointment of Chaceley T Humpidge as General Manager in 1951 was to reverse that. Over the next decade, the trolleybus system was to expand and, whilst no wholly new vehicles were acquired, the acquisition of second-hand vehicles resulted in a much-expanded fleet.

Policy was to change again following the appointment of John Wake as General Manager in 1961; with city redevelopment planned, he found the Transport Committee willing to sanction trolleybus conversion. Although he remained only a year before being replaced by Edward Deakin, John Wake effectively sealed the fate of the trolleybus.

During the 1960s, the bus fleet grew as a result both of trolleybus conversion as well as the introduction of new routes, such as the joint services to Halifax and to Eldwick with Halifax Corporation and West Yorkshire RCC respectively. By 1970, the trolleybus fleet had declined to some 70 vehicles, overshadowed by a bus fleet that now numbered some 260. A further 90 buses were delivered between 1970 and 1972, with the final vehicles to arrive being 20 Alexander-bodied Daimler Fleetlines.

The deeper front windscreens of the later East Lancs bodies fitted to Bradford's second-hand trolleybus acquisitions gave the body a more up-to-date appearance. It was, however, destined to be a short-lived development as, under the brief managership of John Wake, policy was changed when, as in his previous post at St Helens, he pressed for trolleybus abandonment. Fleet number 831 was one of five BUT chassis from a total of six acquired from Doncaster but which had started life with Darlington Corporation in 1949. Here it is heading through the redeveloped The Tyrls, as Town Hall Square had recently been renamed, with the impressive City Hall in the background. Conversion of the Clayton route to motorbus operation at the end of July 1971 caused 831's withdrawal, shortly after this photograph was taken. *Roy Marshall*

This fine view of Forster Square before its redevelopment features 622, one of the city's many long-lived trolleybuses, bound for Saltaire, a regular intermediate short-working on the trunk route serving Manningham Lane. One of 15 AEC 661Ts delivered in 1935, with English Electric bodies, in 1946 it was rebodied by Northern Coachbuilders, which rebodied most of this class – it had the first of the two designs supplied by the firm. It ran thus until withdrawal following the conversion of the Bradford Moor route in November 1962. The ongoing redevelopment of the Forster Square area was to lead to the conversion of these cross-city services despite original plans for trolleybus retention and the acquisition of the overhead equipment to facilitate the work. *Travelens/Vic Nutton*

From 1945 to 1957 Bradford's single-deck fleet was just two. Fleet numbers 444/5 were Weymann-bodied AEC Regals new in 1936 and equipped internally as semi-coaches for private hire, committee visits and similar work. The last petrol-engined buses delivered new to Bradford, they were fitted with AEC 7.7-litre diesel engines in 1948, not that this reduced their ability to move at speed. As a result of an accident involving 445, both were fitted with limiters to ensure that the then maximum speed of 30mph was strictly adhered to. *Roy Marshall*

Nine of Bradford's 1934 delivery of 21 English Electric-bodied AEC 661T, mainly intended for conversion of the Thornton tram route, were fitted with new utility bodywork by Brush in 1944; the remainder were later rebodied by Northern Coachbuilders. Brush-rebodied 612 was photographed in April 1957. Despite the destination indicated, the trolleybus is on an enthusiasts' tour and is heading from Toller Lane to Little Lane over the loop opened in 1934 to serve Duckworth Lane depot. *Geoffrey Morant*

In 1945/46 Bradford received a total of 37 Karrier W chassis with utility or semi-utility bodywork by Roe (703-14 and 734-39) and Park Royal (715-33); all were rebodied by East Lancs in the late 1950s. In this April 1957 view at Five Lane Ends, Idle, 731, still with its original body and inbound on route 42 from Greengates, approaches the overhead junction with the 'long-way-round' route from Saltaire via Thackley. A roundabout was later built and the junction layout modified to a full turning-circle, available from all three approaches. In the background is the tractor factory of International Harvester – the site of the Jowett car plant until production ceased in 1954. *Geoffrey Morant*

A feature of the later years of the Bradford fleet was the dedication of specific vehicles for driver training duties and their renumbering into the ancillary vehicle fleet. The first trolleybus to be assigned to this work was Northern Coachbuilders 1948-rebodied 1934 AEC 661T 597, which became the first, 060. Some training was undertaken within the confines of the Bowling works yard, where a special overhead circuit was provided. This April 1957 view, however, is taken at the Bell Dean Road circle, an intermediate turning-point on the Thornton route, where a full circle of wiring was provided. This enabled trainees to become familiar with trolleybus characteristics on the wide but lightly-trafficked outer section of Thornton Road before venturing onto the more involved wiring layouts in the city centre. *Geoffrey Morant*

Outside the city centre, one of the most complex junctions on the trolleybus system was the intersection of Bolton Road and Idle Road. On the left of this June 1970 picture, 745, one of twelve Roe-bodied BUT 9611Ts new in 1949, is turning right from Idle Road into Bolton Road on an inward route 40 journey from Saltaire, its front route number incorrectly set to 45. On the straight-ahead wiring heading for Thornbury depot via Killinghall Road is 785, one of the nine wartime single-deck Karrier Ws acquired from Darlington in 1955/56/57 that were rebodied with forward-entrance double-deck East Lancs bodywork. 785 had an eventful life. Originally a Brush-bodied single-decker acquired from Darlington it entered BCT service in that form, numbered T.403, in January 1957 – an emergency measure caused by diesel fuel shortages resulting from the Suez Crisis. It remained in service thus until withdrawn in January 1958 and was Bradford's last single-deck trolleybus. The emergency over, it was sent to East Lancs for a new front-entrance double-deck body and re-entered service in February 1959. *Michael Russell*

In 1952 Weymann-bodied BUT 758 gained a place in transport history when it became the first UK public service vehicle to be fitted with flashing direction indicators – made possible by a legal quirk by which trolleybuses were not subject to the constraints imposed by the motorbus Construction and Use Regulations. New in 1950 and intended for a new route to Undercliffe which was never completed, it was one of the last batch of trolleybuses purchased new by Bradford. At the time, trolleybus operation was 1.5d per mile more expensive than bus operation and the Corporation tried (unsuccessfully) to cancel the order. The appointment of Chaceley T Humpidge as General Manager in 1951 changed the plans and the trolleybus system's decline was reversed. In this October 1969 picture, 758 has started its ascent to Wibsey along Princes Way and Little Horton Lane, with the recently realigned inward wiring layout via Glydegate just visible to the left. *Geoffrey Morant*

Bradford's first postwar Leylands were 20 8-foot wide Leyland-bodied PD2s, 554-73. Delivered in 1949 they were part of the programme to replace the city's remaining trams. They ran until the late 1960s – the last one was 573, withdrawn in November 1970. This picture is of 560 parked outside Thornbury depot in September 1968.
Alan Mortimer

The Leylands were followed by forty AEC Regent IIIs with Weymann bodywork, new in 1949 and 1950. To avoid the trolleybus fleet numbers in the 600s, the diesel bus fleet numbering recommenced at 1, the few surviving tramcars were renumbered to clear although the end of the city's 4ft 0in gauge network in May 1950 rendered the latter largely irrelevant. Fleet number 17 is awaiting departure in front of the city's main Post Office. Visible on Bolton Road in the background is the central trolleybus wiring loop that encircled BCT's offices, seen on the extreme left. *Geoffrey Morant*

Delivered during 1952 and 1953 East Lancs-bodied AEC Regent IIIs 66-105 had Birmingham-pattern 'new look' fronts. The latter were made and fitted to the chassis by Crossley Motors which had all the necessary jigs from the large batch of bodies it had built for Birmingham. A neat feature on this front and one which would appear on subsequent Bradford buses, was an enamelled badge with the city's crest. The badges were made by Bradford-based jeweller Fattorini & Sons, a company that had come to fame in 1911 when it manufactured the replacement FA Cup (which was won, appropriately, in its inaugural year by Bradford City). Fleet number 75 is pictured in the immediate postwar livery heading past the Alhambra Theatre at the bottom of Morley Street. The grey roof, a legacy of wartime, was changed to blue in 1953/54. *Roy Marshall collection*

11

Chaceley Humpidge renewed the fleet in an ingeniously cost effective way by the judicious acquisition of second-hand vehicles, many of which were then rebodied. The first opportunity was the end of the Notts & Derby system in 1953 from which he bought 17 AEC 661Ts dating from 1937 to 1942 and 15 BUT 9611Ts new in 1949. Numbered 580-596 and 760-774 respectively, they had Weymann bodies, although 587-96 were rebodied by East Lancs before entering service at Bradford – the first of many to be so treated. Number 766 turns ready for departure for Clayton from outside the Town Hall. *Harry Luff/Online Transport Archive*

With two service trolleybuses turning in the loop in Tyrrel Street at the bottom of Sunbridge Road used by vehicles on the Duckworth Lane and Allerton routes, driver trainer 063 turns left from Tyrrel Street onto the section of overhead that gave access to the route towards Thornbury – a section not normally used by vehicles on service. Originally numbered 746 and one of 12 8-foot wide BUT 9611Ts with Roe bodywork new in 1949, 746 was transferred to driver tuition duties and renumbered in December 1966. *Michael Russell*

In 1958 London Transport sold a number of recently overhauled RTs with five-year Certificates of Fitness and Bradford bought 25 to replace wartime utility Daimlers. Numbered 401 to 425, they entered service in what was a Bradford version of London Transport livery, most with small destination apertures and roof number boxes. Taken in 1959, this picture shows Park Royal-bodied 412 and 420 outside the Ritz cinema near the junction of Broadway and Leeds Road. The cinema was integrated within the redevelopment of the Broadway/Forster Square area in the 1960s, closed in 1987 and demolished the following year. *Geoffrey Morant*

The ex-London RTs were later painted in Bradford's standard livery and most were fitted with Bradford's standard destination display. Weymann-bodied RT413 became Bradford 417 and was so treated in March and April 1961. The RTs were withdrawn between 1963 and 1969. *Geoffrey Morant*

13

On a wintry day in March 1969 East Lancs-bodied BUT 801 approaches the complex overhead wiring at Bolton Junction on its way to the city from Saltaire on circuitous route 40. It was one of eight new in 1950/51 which Bradford bought from St Helens when the latter's system closed in 1958 – and General Manager John Wake must have been displeased to encounter them again when he arrived from St Helens in 1961. Before entering service with BCT the vehicles were sent to coachbuilder Roe in Leeds for renovation and modification and, unusually for Bradford's unrebodied second-hand trolleybuses, were fitted with enamelled city crest badges. 801 was one of three that outlasted the remainder by several years and was not withdrawn until December 1970. *Roy Marshall*

In 1958 prewar AEC Regals 445 and 445 were replaced by two AEC Reliances with Roe bodies. Intended to be numbers 106 and 107 they were changed to 301 and 302 before entering service – giving a separate series for single-deckers. Used regularly on private hire work they were delivered in a predominantly cream livery. In April 1967 the two were renumbered 501 and 502. Although based at Ludlam Street garage, 502 is outside Duckworth Lane depot on Sunday morning staff transport duties. The development of the area's tramway system resulted in several small or medium-sized depots on the periphery of the city, each serving a small number of routes, most of which lasted until the end of Bradford City Transport's existence. Duckworth Lane was one; built for the trams, it survived to be the last operational trolleybus depot in 1972. *Michael Russell*

The final extension to the trolleybus network was the spur from the Tong Cemetery route to Holme Wood estate. Unusually for Bradford the overhead terminal wiring at the Dorchester Crescent terminus was the reversing triangle in the background of this picture. During layover time 782's driver takes the opportunity to read his newspaper. Trolleybuses on the two Wakefield Road routes interworked and 782 is actually working service 17; 18 was the number for the Tong Cemetery route. It was one of ten Karrier W new to the Llanelly & District Traction Company in 1945/46. When that system closed in 1952 the chassis were bought by Bradford and fitted with new rear-entrance East Lancs bodies. The Holme Wood route was short-lived – the Wakefield Road (A650) routes were converted to diesel operation on 1 April 1967 prior to major upgrading of the A650. *Geoffrey Morant*

East Lancashire Coachbuilders supplied most of the new bodies for Bradford's trolleybuses during the rebodying programme undertaken during Chaceley Humpidge's much admired managership. The first design, fitted to acquisitions from Llanelly & District, some from Notts & Derbyshire and some of Bradford's own wartime and early post-war Sunbeam and Karrier chassis, was of the usual rear-entrance layout. Less usual for city use at the time were the platform doors – the more so in using East Lancs' unique patented sliding arrangement. Safer they may have been but they added to journey times and latterly were seldom used. On 25 June 1971, 1945 Karrier W 719 takes the curve at Laisterdyke junction, turning from Leeds Road into Killinghall Road. *Michael Russell*

The depots that housed the trolleybus fleet were all in the city's suburbs and their tramway origins resulted in internal layouts that were unsuited to buses. Duckworth Lane was a case in point, trolleybuses having to be reversed out into the main thoroughfare to enter service. Its vehicle allocation, however, was noted for smart appearance as here with 721, one of the DKY batch of Karrier Ws that entered service during 1945 and 1946 with utility or semi-utility bodywork, replaced in 1957 and 1959/60 with new East Lancs bodies, 721 getting one of the first forward-entrance ones in 1959. Duckworth Lane was the last all-trolleybus depot in Britain, not receiving its first allocation of diesel buses until November 1971. *Geoffrey Morant*

15

After the HKW-registered AEC Regents there was a gap of six years before further new double-deckers but from 1959 to 1964 120 AEC Regent Vs joined the fleet. All were 30-foot long and had forward-entrance Metro-Cammell bodywork. Numbered 106-225 they replaced many of the early postwar motorbuses and, Chaceley Humpidge having moved to Sheffield, enabled John Wake to push through the first trolleybus conversions. The last 30 were delivered in early 1964, of which 219 is pictured in March 1967 on the 64 service to Huddersfield via Brighouse, jointly operated with Hebble and Huddersfield. *Geoffrey Morant*

In April 1966 fleet number 112, one of the first batch of 15 Metro-Cammell-bodied Regent Vs (106-120, new 1959), was one of three diesel buses repainted in a modified livery. Pictured here in August 1967 heading up Little Horton Lane on a service to Buttershaw, the style did not find favour with the city's councillors and was short-lived. *Roy Marshall*

The end of a showery morning-peak period at Bolton Junction on 10 September 1970 illustrates the first two styles of East Lancs bodies for the trolleybus rebodying programme instigated under Chaceley Humpidge's managership in the 1950s. First in line is 792, one of the single-deck wartime Karrier W chassis acquired from Darlington and fitted with new forward-entrance East Lancs double-deck bodywork in 1958/59. Behind is 719, a 1945-built Karrier W new to Bradford with the initial, rear-entrance style. The cleared site to the right of the trolleybuses was the location of Bolton depot; closed in 1958 it was converted to a supermarket until demolition. *Michael Russell*

Chaceley Humpidge's astute acquisition of trolleybuses from closing systems started in 1953 with the fleet from Notts & Derbys, then came vehicles from Llanelly, Darlington's single deckers, St Helens, Brighton, Hastings, Doncaster, Ashton, Grimsby-Cleethorpes. The final purchase was twelve Sunbeam F4 chassis from the Mexborough and Swinton system in April 1961. Seven (numbered 841-847) were fitted with new East Lancs bodies; as with some of the other acquisitions, the remainder were used for spares. Seen here in Princes Way at the start of its almost continuous climb to Wibsey, 847 was last trolleybus to enter service in Bradford. Edward Deakin, Bradford's final General Manager, took office in January 1963 and had the task of converting the country's last trolleybus operation, which he carried out without the undue haste that had characterised his predecessor. On March 26th 1972 number 843 was Bradford's last service trolleybus with 844 as the formal final vehicle. It was the end of an era in transport in the United Kingdom. *Geoffrey Morant*

Edward Deakin's vehicle preferences showed in the next delivery of motorbuses with 15 Daimler CVG6-30, numbered 226-240, in 1966. Their bodies were basically East Lancs but were built by Neepsend Coachworks, Sheffield, a company established by Cravens Ltd in order to increase capacity following its acquisition of East Lancashire Coachbuilders in 1964. They were followed by 15 Leyland PD3As, 241-255, with similar bodies. When delivered the new Daimlers were allocated to Saltaire and Ludlam Street depots and were a familiar sight on the ex-trolleybus Bradford Moor-Crossflatts corridor. Descending Church Bank, 234 is heading into Forster Square on a 61 from Undercliffe. The 61 was converted into a cross-city route from March 1964 linking Undercliffe with St Enoch's Road Top. *Roy Marshall*

In addition to the 15 Daimler CVG6s and 15 Leyland PD3s, the 1965 vehicle order included similar numbers of Leyland Atlanteans and Daimler Fleetlines. Numbered 256-270 and 271-285, all were bodied by MCW and entered service in 1967, allocated initially to Bowling and Saltaire depots respectively. This picture shows Fleetline 277 approaching the roundabout at Saltaire; on the left is the trolleybus overhead for route 40. *Roy Marshall*

A further 60 buses were ordered in 1967. The double-deckers were a similar mix to the last order – 15 Leyland Atlanteans (286-300), 15 Leyland PD3s (301-315) and 20 Daimler Fleetlines (316-335). They were to have had MCW bodies but the firm warned that it was overloaded and delivery might be long delayed. It bodied the Atlanteans but asked to be relieved of the rest of the order which was transferred to Alexander.

The PD3s arrived some months after the Atlanteans and Fleetlines. Amongst the last PD3s buil, they they replaced the last of the ex-London RTs. The upper picture shows PD3 305 in Hall Ings awaiting departure on a service to Wyke. The lower one is of Fleetline 326 in Leeds on service 72 which was jointly operated by the two cities. *Roy Marshall, Geoffrey Morant*

The other 10 buses of the 1967 order were high-capacity 36ft-long single-deckers to introduce one-man operation, the local trade union having agreed to the one-man operation of single-deck vehicles only. An AEC Swift demonstrator was on loan in October 1967 and was reported as successful but the order was divided – five AEC Swifts (503-507) and five Leyland Panthers (508-512). Only one company, Marshall of Cambridge, tendered for the dual-door bodywork. All were delivered in 1969 and were numbered in the 'single-deck' series. By the time that the vehicles arrived it had been agreed that one-man operation of double-deck buses could begin and, as a result, all ten were effectively redundant from new.

Above The Swifts were often used for private hire work and three, including No 506 illustrated here outside Thornbury depot, were repainted in a reversed livery; all five passed to the PTE. *Nicholas Harris*

Below The Panthers also passed to the PTE but were sold to Chesterfield Corporation in 1975. In this picture, 511 has left Ludlam Street depot, where all 10 were based, and is turning from Hall Ings into Bridge Street to take up service on the 29, one of the services on which the single-deckers operated from new. *Geoffrey Morant*

To complete the trolleybus conversion programme and also increase one-man operation, 70 more double-deck buses were ordered. There were 40 Daimler Fleetlines and 30 Leyland Atlanteans, all with Alexander's restyled body. They had dual doors and were 33ft long. Fleetlines 401-40 entered service between August and December 1970, Atlanteans 441-470, following in July and August 1971. In this picture Fleetline 419 awaits departure from its stop in Hall Ings on the cross-city 15 from Allerton to West Bowling. *Roy Marshall*

Bradford's last new buses were 20 Daimler Fleetlines with Alexander bodywork (336-355) delivered in August 1972. The industry fashion for dual doors had passed and the trend at the time was back to single door. Number 343 has just left the stop in The Tyrls and is going to Clayton. Following the delivery of the batch, the Transport Committee was of the opinion that it had a sufficient fleet to carry it through until the creation of West Yorkshire PTE. This proved optimistic and Bradford had to hire AEC Regent IIIs, Regent Vs and Leyland PD2s from Huddersfield and Halifax early in 1974 to cope with shortages. *Geoffrey Morant*

21

County Motors

The Farrar brothers, Arthur and Brinton, directors of a cotton doubling mill at Waterloo, started trading as the County Bus Service in October 1919. The business was based on providing transport for the miners to the many pits in the Emley, Flockton and Lepton areas. Managed by Alf Gale and J Clegg, the business expanded and a fleet of eighteen Taylor-bodied AECs and Reos finished in a purple livery was in operation by 1926. The following year the company was purchased jointly by the three major companies operating in the area to the east of Huddersfield – Barnsley & District Traction (soon to be renamed Yorkshire Traction), Yorkshire Woollen District of Dewsbury and West Riding Automobile of Wakefield. This unusual partnership which featured two tramway based BET group companies and the independent West Riding was to last until 1968.

New manager Herbert Burgin adopted a livery of dark blue with ivory roofs and window frames and the existing fleet was replaced by Leyland Lions and Tigers. Double deckers first appeared in the fleet in 1944 and two years later an attractive reversed livery of ivory and lighter blue was introduced. In general future vehicle purchasing policy reflected that of the owning partners: single deck buses followed the Yorkshire Traction ('YTC') policy whereas double deckers followed the West Riding policy. Fleet strength was usually 24 and the vehicles were always smartly presented. The company had many long serving employees – indicative of the good relations between management and staff.

During the time period covered by this book County operated four main routes from Huddersfield: Barnsley via Emley; Dewsbury via Kirkheaton; Wakefield direct and Wakefield via Kirkburton and Scissett. All the routes out of Huddersfield followed the Corporation trolleybus route for two miles to Waterloo and local passengers were discouraged by a minimum protective fare.

The independent West Riding company sold out as a result of financial difficulties in 1967 to the state owned Transport Holding Company; a year later the BET group holdings in Yorkshire Traction and Yorkshire Woollen followed suit to bring all three parent companies into common ownership. Thus there was no longer any need for County to exist as a separate entity and from October 1968 its management was taken over by Yorkshire Traction. All the County vehicles were repainted in the Yorkshire Traction red and cream livery and given YTC fleet numbers. The County garage continued in use and YTC eventually transferred their Huddersfield allocation of buses from St Andrew's Road to Waterloo.

One example of the multiple management of the firm was what happened to two of the four Leyland PS2s (83-86) delivered in 1949. They had Roe bodies to the standard BET design of the time. They soon proved too small for the traffic and numbers 85/86 were given new Windover coach bodies in 1954. The year after this 1959 picture of number 83 in the garage yard at Waterloo, it and number 84 were transferred to Yorkshire Traction which rebodied them as highbridge double-deckers. The tower and chimney of Farrar's cotton doubling mill in Wakefield Road can be seen in the background. *Peter Roberts*

County was allocated seven wartime Guy Arabs (64-70). Numbers 65 and 66 had Park Royal bodies, the others Roe. 65/66 were rebodied by the Roe in 1950, as in this 1959 picture. Together with sister vehicle 65, number 66 spent much of its life working the hourly service from Huddersfield to Barnsley via Emley, Flockton and Darton. On County double-deckers the side destination box over the platform contained a roller blind which, as in this picture, invariably showed a blank. *Peter Roberts*

Due to the unseasoned timber used in the construction of most wartime bodies, by 1953 the deterioration of the bodies on wartime Guy Arabs 68-70 was such that it was more cost effective to rebody rather than rebuild, 64 and 67 having been scrapped in 1949. Roe provided the new bodies – to its usual high standards and in this attractive form number 69 is pictured shortly after leaving Dewsbury bus station. The driver is making a hand signal for a right turn into Aldams Road on the return journey via Mirfield and Kirkheaton to Huddersfield. *March 1959 Geoffrey Morant*

Although vehicle purchasing policy for single-decks tended to follow that of Yorkshire Traction and double-deckers that of West Riding, there can have been little discussion about the order for 1950 Leyland-bodied PD2s 87 and 88, as both operators were buying the same model. The bus is still in its original livery with darker blue roof. *Roy Marshall*

Shown departing from the central island platform at Barnsley bus station, fleet number 89 was one of a pair of Roe-bodied Leyland PD2s new in 1952. Three vehicles were required to operate the basic service between Huddersfield and Barnsley with an extra bus for the Saturday short workings to Emley. Useful connections were advertised at Bretton Cross Roads with the Huddersfield – Kirkburton – Wakefield service. At 15 minutes past the hour passengers from, say, Skelmanthorpe on the Wakefield bound bus could change at Bretton for Darton and Barnsley. Similarly passengers from Emley on the Barnsley bound bus could change for Wakefield. In the background is one of Yorkshire Woollen's twelve Weymann 'Fanfare' bodied AEC Reliance coaches. *Peter Roberts*

Vehicle purchasing policy was affected by the joint ownership – double-deckers tended to follow West Riding policy whilst single-deckers were chosen by Yorkshire Traction and were usually to the BET's current design. Thus when West Riding moved from Leylands to Guys in 1955, County's next double-deckers were Roe-bodied Guy Arabs 91-94, new in 1958. When West Riding was sold to the Transport Holding Company in 1967 followed by the BET companies in 1968, there was no need for the separate company and County was absorbed into Yorkshire Traction in October of that year. Photographed in Barnsley bus station in 1969, 'Tracky' 688 was formerly County 94. It retained its County indicators with no number blind. *Roy Marshall*

For many years Lord Street in Huddersfield served as a 'linear bus station' for company buses serving destinations to the east of the town in addition to some local services operated by Huddersfield Joint Omnibus Committee. Against a backdrop of Huddersfield Parish Church 96 awaits departure at the Dewsbury stand. Delivered in 1959, 96 was one of a pair of Willowbrook-bodied Leyland PSUC1s. They were the first buses in the fleet suitable for one person operation and also its first single-deckers to feature route number indicators although such were never displayed. Originally the number box carried a 'CM' logo, painted on the inside of the glass, as on sister vehicle 95, photographed at Waterloo in reversed livery. *Linden Edwards (96), Photobus (95)*

Photographed in August 1967 when only one month old, this was the penultimate bus in the County fleet. Marshall-bodied Leyland Leopard 114 is negotiating the Shore Head roundabout at Aspley near the end of its 77-minute journey. The blind had already been set for the return journey from Huddersfield to Wakefield. This route was not tightly timed and within a year a triangular yellow plate was affixed to the front of 114 (and sister bus 115) to denote one person operation. This route was known to the crews as 'Wakefield KB' but, more officially, 'route No. 7' by the management. *Alan Mortimer*

West Riding caused County to add two Guy Wulfrunians to its fleet,
their Roe bodies to the same design as West Riding's own. New in 1961
and numbered 99, 100, after some 18 months of trouble, the BET
forced West Riding to take them off County's hands. In the first picture
the pair are passing in Flockton on 28th April 1963 – their last day in
service with County. They were then moved to West Riding, which
fitted its own pattern of indicators, repainted them green and
numbered them 995/96. In the smaller picture, 996 is on a local
Pontefract service in July 1965. *Geoff Lumb Alan Mortimer*

The Wulfrunians were replaced by a pair of
Roe-bodied Leyland PD3As, (105/06). Purchased
in 1964, they were the last new double deckers in
the County fleet. Negotiating the Bull Ring shortly
after departure from Wakefield bus station in July
1965, 105 heads for its home town via Flockton
and Lepton. This hourly service required two
vehicles and the two newest highbridge deckers
were the usual allocation. Known as 'Wakefield
Direct' by the passengers, 'Straight Wakefield' by
the crews and 'service No 1' by the management,
this flagship route for many years required
duplication on Saturdays. *Alan Mortimer*

Halifax

Halifax's electric trams commenced operation in 1898 and by 1904 an extensive network was in operation although there were no joint workings to Bradford or Huddersfield due to the differences in gauge. Motor bus operation started in October 1912 with Daimler single-deckers. A joint service between Halifax and Huddersfield was established in 1925 and, following a Ministry of Transport inquiry, Hebble was also granted a licence to operate on this route. 1926 saw a short-lived service operated by Halifax and Rochdale Corporations between the two towns.

Ben Hall arrived from Wigan to be manager in 1921 and introduced a trolleybus service using two Railless vehicles acquired from Dundee; an additional Tilling Stevens trolleybus was purchased in 1924. Hall left to become manager at Portsmouth, where he introduced an extensive trolleybus network. His successor, Walter Young, had scrapped trolleybuses in Dundee and quickly did the same in Halifax. From 1926 to 1929 vehicle purchases were Karriers, built in Huddersfield. The first double-deckers – AECs – arrived in 1929 and AEC would be the choice for single- and double-deckers until after the Second World War. Reputedly following the inspection of a bus in Glasgow Corporation livery, a similar orange, green and cream livery was adopted from 1929, although trams continued to be maroon and cream until their end in February 1939.

In 1928 an approach was made by the London Midland & Scottish Railway ('LMS') and the London & North Eastern Railway companies for the joint working of services in the area. This resulted in the LMS, taking over the Halifax – Rochdale service, and the railway companies were granted licenses for four other Halifax services. On 1st April 1929 the Halifax Joint Omnibus Committee ('JOC') was formed by the Corporation and the railway companies; services were then divided into three categories:

A – *Services within the borough boundary, to be operated by Halifax Corporation.*
B – *Services beyond the borough boundary but terminating within the suburban area would be worked by the Corporation for the Joint Omnibus Committee ('JOC')*
C – *Long distance services extending beyond the B services which would be operated entirely by the railways or their nominees.*

The Halifax fleet ownership, income and costs would be divided according to this. The following month the railway companies purchased Hebble and in 1932 the C services passed to Hebble although the LMS continued to operate the Rochdale service until December 1933.

After the war the undertaking had four general managers, two of whom – Roderick Mackenzie and Geoffrey Hilditch – would later play important roles in the industry. Situated on the edge of the Pennines, Halifax's operating territory was particularly hilly and each manager's approach to this was reflected in vehicle purchases of variously AECs, Leylands and Daimlers for the fleet of around 170. After extensive trials with several demonstrators the first

Very steep hills were a feature of Halifax services as in this picture of AEC Reliance 261 which, having travelled from Burnley, is just about to leave Lee Wood Road and join Heptonstall Road for the steep descent to the Calder valley at Bankfoot. One of two with Plaxton dual-purpose bodies purchased in 1971, it was operating the Burnley – Halifax – Leeds service 8. Normally routed along the Calder valley, on this particular date in April 1972 there was an emergency road closure in the valley at Charlestown and the service had been diverted 'over the top' following the route of former Hebble service 15 to Leeds. Just visible below the centre nearside window is a slip board giving the main places on the route. *John Kaye*

Eight AEC Regent III's with London Transport RT chassis were delivered in 1946, their Roe bodies to that firm's standard design of the period. In this 1959 view with the Town Hall tower and clock in the background number 32 is climbing Broad Street, the semaphore arm trafficator indicating that the vehicle was about to make a right turn into Crossfield Bus Station. *Jim Thompson*

rear-engined vehicles arrived in 1966 – Daimler Fleetlines with Northern Counties bodywork which became Halifax's standard for double-deckers, apart from the last five Dennis Lolines built, in 1967.

The railway interests in the Joint Committee and ownership of Hebble passed to the National Bus Company in January 1969 and, as part of a rationalisation programme, on 1st March 1971 most of the Hebble stage services in the area were taken over by the JOC, together with a number of vehicles. On 6th September 1971 the vehicles and services of the Todmorden Joint Omnibus Committee also passed to the Halifax JOC and a new body, the Calderdale Joint Omnibus Committee, was formed although in effect it was a takeover of Todmorden by Halifax. In practice the two changes took place progressively over the period February to September, for example Halifax vehicles working Hebble services before the March 1st, revisions to Todmorden's operations in August, early repainting into Halifax livery and various vehicle loans. The new JOC was not long lived – as a result of local government reorganisation, on 1st April 1974 Halifax Corporation Transport and the Calderdale JOC became part of the West Yorkshire Passenger Transport Executive.

There was continual renumbering as vehicles were transferred between the corporation ('A') and Joint Omnibus Committee ('JOC' or 'B') fleets. Pictured on Furness Drive, Illingworth, Park Royal-bodied AEC Regent III number 31, new in 1947, was originally 217 in the Halifax JOC fleet transferring to the Corporation fleet in 1954. The typical Halifax bus of the period, there were 73 of this design in the fleets, including 16 of eight-foot width. Unique to Halifax, the timber frame was based on Park Royal's wartime body rather than its post-war steel-framed design and it proved an unwise choice. For reasons of economy the specification was pared down – too much, for it led to severe structural weaknesses which were to become the bane of the department's body shop's life for years to come. *Arthur Wilson*

In 1947/48 Halifax purchased nine Leyland PD2/1s with Leyland bodywork. Originally numbered 335-343, they later became 100-108, as in this picture of 108 taken in 1959. It was the only one of the batch to be later transferred to the JOC fleet, becoming 308. Upon withdrawal in 1965 it and three others were sold to Oldham Corporation to assist with a serious shortage of vehicles, being repainted for Oldham by the Halifax paint shop. *Geoffrey Morant*

In April 1963 Roe-bodied AEC Regent III 56 is pictured at the stop outside the head office of the Halifax Building Society in Commercial Street, awaiting departure on the short route to the General Hospital. It was one of four AEC Regent IIIs with Roe bodywork delivered to the Corporation in 1948. Originally numbered 305-308, they became 53-56 in 1952. Four similar vehicles (213-216) joined the JOC fleet. *Roy Marshall*

New in 1951 fleet number 77, originally 357, was one of the Halifax's final batch of six Park Royal-bodied AEC Regent IIIs. Unlike the previous batches, these had steel-frames to a design based upon the styling of London's RT body. This April 1963 photograph was taken in Powell Street most likely whilst the crew was on layover – Powell Street was the location of the Inspectors' office and staff canteen. All six were withdrawn in 1966/67. The revised indicator style was introduced by new general manager Roderick Mackenzie. *Roy Marshall*

Two batches of Roe-bodied AEC Regal IIIs (251-269) joined the Joint Committee fleet in 1949. Most of these were converted in the Halifax bodyshop in 1953/4 to front entrance to enable one-man operation. This view shows 259 on route 46 from the Pennine hilltop village of Heptonstall to Halifax. The road up to Heptonstall was a steep and narrow, its junction with the main road along the valley at Hebden Bridge, involved a sharp back right 150 degree turn when coming from Halifax. Far too tight for any large vehicle, buses had to run past the junction and reverse into Church Lane so as to face the junction and ascend the hill. Vice versa coming down, as in this picture of 259 which has come down the hill onto the main road and is about to reverse into Church Lane, with Bankfoot Mill in the background. A turning circle was later constructed just beyond where the photographer was standing, eliminating this somewhat risky manoeuvre. *Arthur Wilson*

Left Roddie Mackenzie left for Edinburgh early in 1956 and the new manager, from Bury, was Richard le Fevre one of whose first actions was a livery experiment. On 8th August number 285 emerged from the workshops with the orange and green reversed, as in this view taken in Hollins Lane, Mixenden (shown as Wheatley on the blinds). It did not meet with approval and soon reverted to standard layout. The bus was one of ten Daimler CVG6 with Metro-Cammell bodies delivered in 1954. *Arthur Wilson*

Below A previous simplification of the livery, made by MacKenzie, was even less liked. *Roy Marshall*

Daimler's CD650 model was something of an 'almost right' and there were very few examples in the United Kingdom. The 10.6-litre Daimler engine, large for its time, was just what was needed for Halifax hills but the over complex high pressure hydraulics of the braking, steering and gearchange systems proved a nightmare. In 1951 Halifax bought six with East Lancashire 8ft-wide bodywork – the only East Lancs bodies bought new by Halifax. Although the bodies were the opposite of the hydraulics all were withdrawn in 1962 and sold for scrap. Numbered 349-354 (and later 81-86) this May 1961 view shows number 85 at the junction of Stainland Road and Saddleworth Road in West Vale. The trolleybus overhead was for the Huddersfield Corporation service from West Vale via Huddersfield to Almondbury. *Travelens/Vic Nutton*

Opposite top Twelve Daimler CVG6 with teak-framed Roe bodies arrived in 1954. Numbered 87-98 (90 is shown here) in the Corporation fleet they became a problem when a combination of hills, heavy bodies and a creosote-based fuel additive caused excessive wear in their 8.4-litre Gardner 6LW engines. Manager Dick le Fevre had a drastic solution which made them unique when in 1956/57 he fitted them with Leyland O.600 engines. Later, under another general manager, Gardner was persuaded to supply a 10.45-litre 6LX which replaced the O.600 in number 95. *Roy Marshall*

Opposite bottom Hills also meant flash floods and 117 is seen here negotiating such a flood at Cote Hill on the 27th June 1970. One of five Daimler CVG6 with Roe bodies which had teak lower-deck and aluminium upper-deck frames, the result being lighter than the previous 12. They were the last buses ordered by general manager MacKenzie and also the last new Halifax buses with rear platforms. They would have an extended life in the fleet due to the acquisition of Hebble's bus services and the Todmorden undertaking. Another change, introduced in the search for reduced costs and additional sources of income was external advertising; the fleet number was moved to the lower nearside corner of the panel. *Don Akrigg*

Mills and hills were a feature of the landscape. Here in February 1967, having just descended Salterhebble Hill, is Halifax 117 a Roe-bodied Daimler CVG6. *Arthur Wilson*

Opposite top Halifax's first underfloor-engined vehicles arrived in 1958 and Dick Le Fevre's vehicle preferences were straightforward – Leyland chassis and MCW-group bodies. What was unusual was that these nine Weymann-bodied single-deckers were Leyland Worldmasters. The Worldmaster was primarily an export model and Halifax was one of only a few home market operators to purchase it. They started a new numbering series (1-9) and this is the first, number 1, in July 1969 outside what was always known as 'The Halifax' on Commercial Street, on the cross town service from Northowram to the General Hospital. *Roy Marshall*

Opposite bottom Although there were sixteen AEC Regent V – a picture of one is on the front cover of this book – the other orders went to Leyland. After eight PD3s in 1959, the Regents were matched by sixteen PD2s, all with Metro Cammell bodies, the deliveries of the PD2s and Regents divided equally between the corporation and JOC fleets. In this July 1969 view taken at Queensbury, JOC-owned PD2 221's driver reads his newspaper in the break before the return journey to Halifax. In the background is Hebble 275 an AEC Regent V with lowbridge Weymann bodywork on the through service from Bradford to Halifax. Bradford Corporation also operated a service from Bradford which terminated at Queensbury; when Hebble's bus operations passed to Halifax in February 1971 the service became jointly operated by Halifax and Bradford, bringing Bradford vehicles into Halifax for the first time. *Linden Edwards*

35

Joint Committee-owned Leyland Leopard 231 was unique in the fleet. New in 1961, its high capacity Weymann body had front entrance and centre exit doors, 34 seats and space for 24 standing passengers. As with many 'odd one outs' it proved unpopular and in 1964 the centre door was removed and the seating altered to 42. *Roy Marshall*

After the demonstration of a Maidstone & District Albion Nimbus, the JOC placed an order for ten of the updated NS3AN model with Weymann bodies, planning to use them on the routes to the upland villages along the Calder Valley – Cragg Vale, Midgley, Booth and Heptonstall, recasting the services as feeders to the main valley services. Numbered 250-259 they entered service in 1963. Richard le Fevre retired in 1963 and the idea was an unwelcome part of the legacy which he left for his successor, Geoffrey Hilditch. He had been engineer to MacKenzie and Le Fevre before moving to Plymouth as deputy and then general manager at Great Yarmouth, and was one of a group of young general managers who would have considerable influence on the industry. In this May 1965 picture 257, bound for Heptonstall (its destination blind has slipped), is about to turn round so as to be able to ascend Heptonstall Road – the sharp junction can just be seen at the extreme right. Cutting the through services would not have worked, the Nimbuses were not reliable and Geoffrey Hilditch sold them in 1965, 1966 and 1967. *Arthur Wilson*

Another legacy was an order for 30 more Weymann-bodied Leyland PD2s, placed just before Geoff Hilditch took over and about which he was not best pleased. A strike at Weymann's works caused some of the 30 PD2 chassis to be 'frozen' there until matters were resolved. Ten of the other chassis were sent to Roe at Leeds. Two entered service in the JOC fleet (278-279) and eight in the Corporation fleet (59-66). These entered service in 1965 and were the first with Geoff Hilditch's revised indicator layout. This picture is of a shiny new 62 at School Lane, Illingworth. *Linden Edwards*

The Weymann strike forced the stop-gap purchase of five 1947/48 Roe-bodied AEC Regents from Leeds City Transport – two went into the Corporation fleet and the others to the JOC. None received Halifax livery, cream paint simply being applied over the former light green area of the Leeds livery. This picture is of 422 at King Cross bound for Midgley in November 1964 – the road layout was later completely changed. *Arthur Wilson*

The vehicle shortage prompted the 1965 acquisition of two single-deckers from the Sheffield Joint Omnibus Committee. Numbered 19 and 20 in the Corporation fleet they were integrally constructed AEC Monocoaches – AEC running units in a Park Royal-built frame. New in 1955 they had been Sheffield 1205/06; transferred to the Halifax JOC fleet in 1967 and renumbered 219/220 they were withdrawn in 1969. The picture, on the return journey from Siddal, shows the unusual way in which the lettering of the destination for the town's bus station was arranged with a curved lower edge to the word Crossfield – a feature of the blinds for many years. *Arthur Wilson*

After extensive trials with rear-engined and other double-deckers, Geoffrey Hilditch standardised on the Gardner-engined Daimler Fleetline. He would have preferred Roe for the bodies but Northern Counties' body was of slightly lower overall height and would fit with good clearance under a critical low bridge in Field Lane, Brighouse. A total of 45 joined the two fleets over the years 1966-1972; number 89 was one of seven delivered to the corporation fleet in 1970 and in this June 1971 view is leaving Crown Street, Hebden Bridge. The 30-ft long AEC Regent V behind was one of eight delivered to the JOC in 1960 which, along with the 1958 PD3s, provided the vehicle requirement for the long Hebden Bridge to Brighouse service until conversion to one man operation in 1973. *Geoffrey Morant*

Oldham-based Seddon's bodybuilding division, Pennine, supplied the bodies for seven AEC Reliances in 1966. General Manager Geoffrey Hilditch had worked for Seddon early in his career and had bought their bodywork when in charge at Great Yarmouth. They were numbered 249-255 in the JOC fleet; this picture shows the last of the batch on service 50 in Cain Lane, Southrowram. *Nicholas Harris*

Besides the double-deck Fleetlines, in 1968/69 Halifax bought nine of the 33ft-long single-deck model – seven with Willowbrook bodies and two by Pennine. Here, brand new Willowbrook-bodied 112 is leaving Halifax town centre along Portland Place, heading for Skircoat Road en-route to the General Hospital. The flip-up sign in the windscreen informed passengers when concessionary fares were available. *Linden Edwards*

The JOC's purchase of five Dennis Lolines – the last built for the UK market – was something about which the general manager admitted later that maybe his heart had ruled his head. Bodied by Northern Counties, they were delivered to the JOC in 1967, numbered 300–304 and had coach seating. Heart or head they proved very useful for private hire and a contract for transporting workers from the South Yorkshire coal mining area to the Meredith & Drew biscuit factory in Halifax, their low height making them very suitable for this type of operation. They were sold to West Riding in 1970 to help replace Wufrunians there but there was later some regret about this as they would have been useful when Halifax took over Todmorden with its low height garage. In this March 1967 picture brand new 301 is climbing from Elland to Ainley Top on the jointly-operated service to Huddersfield. *Arthur Wilson*

After trials with more demonstration vehicles Geoffrey Hilditch had ordered three Seddon RU's with Plaxton bus bodies with coach seating. Delivered in 1970 and numbered 315-317 in the 'B' (JOC) fleet, their 'reversed' livery with cream lower panels looked smart. This view of 316 was taken at Dudley Hill in April 1971 on the Halifax – Odsal – Dudley Hill – Stanningley – Leeds service which was operated by Halifax from 22nd February 1971, a week before the formal change date and this bus had operated the first journey. In August, as part of the Todmorden merger, service 8 was extended through Hebden Bridge and Todmorden to Burnley. *John Kaye*

On 1st March 1971, as part of a National Bus Company area reorganisation, many of Hebble's stage services passed to Halifax and one result of this was that Halifax buses started to run to Rochdale once again. In this March 1974 picture, number 9, one of ten Plaxton-bodied Leyland Leopards bought in 1972/73, is leaving Rochdale for Leeds. As with the 8 service shown in the previous picture, the change to working by Halifax took place on 22nd February – a week before the formal transfer date. *Geoffrey Morant*

As part of the transfer of Hebble, Halifax acquired a number of Hebble's AEC Regents and Reliances – some were repainted, others, which only ran for a day or so, were not. Above, climbing Keighley Road, Illingworth, with a good load of passengers is Halifax 76, a Northern Counties-bodied AEC Regent V new to Hebble in 1962; it had been Hebble 619. Below, at Bank Top, Southrowram, is Park Royal-bodied AEC Reliance 318, formerly Hebble 660. *Linden Edwards, Nicholas Harris*

The Halifax JOC absorbed the Todmorden undertaking in September 1971, the merged result being renamed the Calderdale Joint Omnibus Committee. Informally, this had been more or less in place since Todmorden's long serving general manager, Ted Metcalfe, retired in the Spring of that year. Halifax's order for twelve new Fleetlines was increased to seventeen and nine were allocated to Todmorden – the lower height Northern Counties body enabled them to operate from Millwood Depot. The Halifax coat of arms and fleetname was omitted, anticipating the formation of the West Yorkshire Passenger Transport Executive on 1st April 1974. In July 1972, new Fleetline 297 is about to depart from the Market Ground bus station in Todmorden. *Roy Marshall*

There was a general delay in the delivery of Fleetline chassis and to bridge the gap four lightweight AEC Regent Vs with Park Royal bodies were bought from a dealer – the sale of the Lolines became a matter of regret. Originally with Maidstone & District the Regents arrived in January 1972 and, numbered 361-364, ran in their Maidstone livery. Two had lowbridge bodies and were allocated to Todmorden – the low roof of the depot at Millwood depot is clear in this picture. They were the only vehicles in the Halifax fleet to have rear-platform doors. *John Kaye*

A condition of the merger with Todmorden was that the average age of the acquired fleet would be brought up to that of the Halifax JOC. To achieve this, in August 1971 three Marshall-bodied Leopards were bought from Yorkshire Traction and two Fleetlines from Yorkshire Woollen. One of the latter had been new to Hebble in 1966 and was of similar design to the Halifax ones – its picture is in the Hebble section of this book. The other was this Alexander-bodied one, seen at Bull Green roundabout in Halifax town centre on the frequent service to Mixenden. New to Yorkshire Woollen, it was transferred to Hebble to provide a pair for the Bradford to Huddersfield service. In the March 1971 Hebble reorganisation both passed to Woollen and were then sold to Halifax in August. Too high to fit into Todmorden's Millwood garage, it was put into the Corporation fleet as 103, the existing (and lower height) Northern Counties-bodied103 moving to the JOC fleet as 293. *Roy Marshall*

Pictured near Crossfield Bus Station on 21st April 1972 working the former Hebble service 28 to Rochdale, Burlingham-bodied Leyland Leopard 309 was a much-travelled vehicle. It was new to the Sheffield C fleet (railway owned) in 1960, passing to Yorkshire Woollen in February 1970, Halifax JOC acquired it and sister vehicle 308 from Yorkshire Woollen in February 1971 and three similar ones (305-307) from Hebble, as part of the reorganisation. *John Kaye*

Hanson

Mary Hanson started a horse drawn carriers business as early as the 1830s specialising in carrying both textiles and textile machinery for the local woollen mills in the Colne Valley. In due course this developed into long distance haulage with regular journeys to London. Natural diversification led to a fleet of Leyland charabancs being advertised for private hire and excursions to Blackpool by 1920. Four years later the first bus service was inaugurated linking the villages of Golcar and Linthwaite on opposite sides of the Colne Valley and making connection with the Corporation trams on Manchester Road. Huddersfield Watch Committee refused licences for further service developments into Huddersfield which were operated on the return ticket system.

By 1929 the Blue and White Bus Service operated by Walter Bower along Manchester Road to Marsden was providing stiff competition for the Corporation tram service as were Hanson's buses on the Slaithwaite service. Rather strangely, the Corporation and Hanson jointly bought the Blue and White service agreeing to share the Marsden bus route on an equal basis. As part of the deal the Hanson routes to Slaithwaite and Heights were also pooled but in return the Corporation granted Hanson the necessary licences so that all their services could operate on a fully legal basis.

By 1938 the Huddersfield Joint Omnibus Committee ('JOC') was convinced of the necessity of either the outright purchase of the Hanson services or of the extension of the existing Colne Valley coordination scheme to include all the services in the Golcar area. The JOC would not accept Robert Hanson's lowest price and so the coordination scheme ('CVS') came into effect from September 1939. The other Hanson routes – Meltham via Helme; Oldham via Uppermill and the two from Lindley to Newsome and Huddersfield respectively were excluded from the deal.

The Hanson bus fleet usually consisted of about two dozen vehicles – originally Leylands, later AECs predominated. The first double deckers appeared in 1933 and some vehicles classified as dual purpose would supplement the much larger coach fleet as required. The rebuilding programme in later years added great variety to the fleet. Chief Engineer Jim Holmes and his staff gained an excellent reputation for re-conditioning and re-working the chassis from old buses and coaches before fitting them with new Roe bus bodies. By allocating new chassis numbers the Huddersfield licensing authorities were persuaded to give these buses new registrations and, together with new fleet numbers, the public were convinced that these really were new buses. Seven 'new' double deckers were created along with fifteen single deckers suitable for one man operation.

By the end of 1968 even though the stage-carriage side of the business was still profitable, with all but three of the fleet being rebuilds of previous stock , expensive fleet replacement would soon be inevitable. Consequently James Hanson (later Lord Hanson) explained that they had reluctantly decided to sell out to the Corporation. Following the 1968 Transport Act the Corporation had renewed their interest in purchasing the Hanson business and a purchase price was agreed. Thus almost 45 years of local bus operation ceased and from 1 October 1969 Hanson's Buses Ltd became a coach operator only.

New in 1948, fleet number 249 was one of a pair of 1948 Duple-bodied Albion CX13, seen here in October 1960 loading outside the main Huddersfield Co-operative building on Buxton Road, Huddersfield – a popular stop which saved the long walk from the main shopping area to the bus station. Originally the body had a white band below the windows and a larger destination box. The bus is operating the Saturday-only 'Linthwaite Church flyer' – so called because the round trip was tightly timed at 30 minutes to give an even headway between the half-hourly Meltham via Linthwaite Church service buses. From 1962 this vehicle found a new life in the Hanson Driving School.

From 1949 Hanson had only four double-decker buses – three AEC Regents (285-87) and a wartime Guy Arab (183) – the buses were numbered in the same series as Hanson's coaches. By 1955 the Guy had reached the end of the road, added to which the Huddersfield Joint Omnibus Committee, with whom Hanson jointly operated the Colne Valley services, was planning to re-route the Golcar Circulars to avoid the 'low mill' in Grove Street which had previously prevented the use of double deckers. Rather than purchase new double-deckers Hanson's chief engineer, Jim Holmes, was asked to rebuild several older single-deck chassis and fit them with new Roe bodies. Completed in 1956 347 was the first to appear utilising the running units from a 1938 AEC Regal coach and parts of another Regal from Chapman's Ivy Coaches. The completed vehicles were given new registration numbers and Hanson's own chassis numbers. Often used on the Hill Top and Wilberlee route, 347 is pictured in September 1962 at the Hill Top terminus. *Geoff Lumb*

The second Hanson rebuild entered service in December 1957 incorporating running units from 245, a 1948 AEC Regal III coach, and again a new registration number. Number 349 is shown leaving the bus station in October 1968 on the service to Meltham via Milnsbridge and Helme. Manchester Street was closed for the construction of the new Civic Centre and consequently the driver was about to make a left turn into Macaulay Street in order to proceed via High Street to the first outward stop in Buxton Road. *Geoffrey Morant*

During the early 1960s economics dictated that more services should be converted to one-man operation particularly Hanson's own routes to Lindley and Newsome which were single-deck operated. Again it was left to the engineering department to provide suitable buses by re-building eight older AEC Regal chassis, over the years 1960-1963, fitting them with new Roe full-fronted bodies. Nicknamed 'Tanks' the bodies had no bulkhead behind the driver, who had to twist through 90 degrees to issue tickets from a Setright machine. On a foggy day 363 is seen at the Weatherhill Road, Lindley terminus, on the edge of the moors about two miles north west of the town centre. *Nicholas Harris*

By 1961 double-deckers had appeared on both the Slaithwaite and two of the Scapegoat Hill routes and this coupled with the advancing age of the three 1949 Regents meant there was an urgent need for replacements. The result, over a three-year period, was four more Hanson/AEC/Roe rebuilds. The penultimate example, 370, appeared in 1962 and it is pictured here climbing up Morley Lane out of Milnsbridge on the hilly route to Meltham. The textile mills so typical of the Colne Valley scenery at the time provided many of the passengers at the start and finish of shifts. *Nicholas Harris*

The final double-deck rebuild of 1963, Roe-bodied AEC-Hanson Regent III, actually incorporated running units from 287, one of the three 1949 Regents. Operating a joint Colne Valley service to Slaithwaite via Paddock Head, Milnsbridge and Wellhouse, it is pictured here in April 1967 just outside the bus station at the junction of Swallow Street and Upperhead Row where it will make a left turn and leave Town via Trinity Street. A Huddersfield bus on the same route would have displayed route number 6 but Hanson never felt the need to display such numbers.
Geoffrey Morant

The gleaming structure of the new Civic Centre in the background contrasts with the drab appearance of 377 which is badly in need of a repaint. Five years old when this picture was taken in October 1968, it was the last of the AEC-Hanson rebuilds of Regents and Regals. Shown in the 'Top' or Upperhead Row bus station the lightly loaded bus awaits departure time on the joint Colne Valley service to Scapegoat Hill. The route, via Paddock Head, Milnsbridge, Golcar and Bolster Moor, numbered 3 by the JOC, involved steep gradients and tight bends before it reached the moorland village terminus, 5 miles west of Huddersfield and a climb of some 750ft. *Geoffrey Morant*

From 1964 the AEC Regal IVs, new in 1952 and the AEC Reliances of 1954 which had served as one man vehicles were in need of replacement. This led to the final programme of rebuilding, this time involving seven former AEC Reliance coaches, the vehicles again getting new registration numbers and new Roe bodies. Here in July 1968 rebuilt Reliance 389 of 1965 is at Clough Head on the joint Colne Valley service to Scapegoat Hill via Manchester Road and Leymoor Road. *Geoff Lumb*

One of two 36-ft long Willowbrook-bodied AEC Reliances which entered service in 1967 is pictured two years later about to set out on the long journey over the Pennines to Oldham via Marsden, Standedge and Uppermill. Hanson had operated this service since 1930 but passenger numbers had decreased drastically with the result that on weekdays from April 1968 only three return trips were offered and even then the seating capacity of this vehicle would not be fully utilised. Following the sale of the stage carriage side of the business to Huddersfield Corporation, on the final day of operation, Tuesday 30th September 1969, at 11.50pm 405 was recorded as being the last bus to enter the St John's Road Garage. *Roy Marshall*

The Hanson bus fleet and services passed to the corporation in October 1969. Former Hanson 382, a 1964 Roe-bodied AEC Reliance Hanson rebuild, is shown here in 1972 repainted in Huddersfield livery and renumbered 82. It is working the former Hanson route from Huddersfield to Weatherhill Road, Lindley via Birkby – the only Hanson route to pass the firm's garage on St John's Road. The bus is turning from Northumberland Street into John William Street in front of the former Corporation Transport Head Office. Originally given the route number 96 by the Corporation by April 1970 it had become part of routes 92/93 linking Ainley Top/Weatherhill via Birkby, Town, Fernside, Newsome, Milnsbridge and Lindley. *Roy Marshall*

Had it not been for two serious fires on Standedge during 1967, one of which destroyed one of the AEC Regal IVs, Willowbrook-bodied AEC Reliances 405/06 would most likely have been the last two service buses purchased by Hanson. The fires left the company short of a suitable vehicle and a further similar Reliance had to be bought. Numbered 412 it entered service in May 1968, the corporation numbering it 3 when it acquired Hanson's bus fleet some 18 months later. *Nicholas Harris*

Hebble

The Hebble business was formed by brothers Oliver and Charles Holdsworth on 1st December 1924. The family had many and varied business interests in the area and the brothers had already commenced running motor charabancs as an offshoot to their haulage business. Failure to obtain licences to operate local stage carriage routes locally resulted in them forming the Bilton Motor Company in 1922 to provide services in the Harrogate area which they sold to the Harrogate & District Company some two years later.

The first manager was Norman Dean – a nephew of the Holdsworths – who managed the short-lived Bilton operation and who would then guide Hebble through a period of expansion until he left in 1939 to become general manager of Yorkshire Traction. The first operating base was at Wards End, Halifax, on land owned by the Holdsworths. With the expanding fleet a depot and offices were established at Walnut Street, Halifax, in August 1927. With the acquisition of the J W North haulage business in Bradford a depot became available at Legrams Lane in Bradford and when the railway companies took over, new accommodation was provided at Edderthorpe Street, Bradford. In 1942 a depot and offices were constructed at Park Lane, Bradford, on land purchased from the railway companies, used by Hebble and Yorkshire Woollen District until its closure in 1969.

The London Midland and Scottish Railway, having obtained operating powers in August 1928, commenced a service from Rochdale to Halifax, this being a prelude to purchasing Hebble in early 1929 jointly with the London and North Eastern Railway. In May of that year an agreement was reached between the railway companies and Halifax Corporation to split the local route network into three categories.

A – Services operated only by Halifax Corporation.

B – Services operating to an agreed outer suburban area – the Halifax Joint Omnibus Committee

C – Long distance services to be operated by the railway company – Hebble.

Seven Hebble services passed to the Halifax JOC. In February 1932 the BET purchased the railway companies' interests but the above agreement would continue until March 1971. The BET interests passed to the National Bus Company in January 1969 and some of Yorkshire Woollen's Halifax area services were moved to Hebble. However this was not long lasting and in the wider reorganisation of March 1971 some of Hebble's stage services and bus fleet were transferred to the Halifax JOC, the remainder passing to Yorkshire Woollen. Hebble's excursions, tours and express services continued, under the management of Yorkshire Woollen, until January 1974 when the company name was changed to National Travel East.

Prior to the Second World War vehicle purchases comprised mostly Leylands and Albions, and post war most of its fleet of around 85 were BET-standard Leylands and AECs.

Photographed on 5th June 1961 in Chester Street Bus Station, Bradford, 267 was is one of four AEC Regent IIIs with lowbridge bodywork by Willowbrook. When delivered in 1952 these vehicles had crash gearboxes, replaced soon after delivery with synchromesh units. In the background is 192 a Park Royal-bodied AEC Reliance on route 26 to Hipperholme. Hebble shared a depot with Yorkshire Woollen at Park Avenue in Bradford – it closed in October 1969, Hebble vehicles transferring to the West Yorkshire depot in Hammerton Street.
John Kaye

In 1949 two batches of AEC Regent IIIs with Roe lowbridge bodywork were delivered – three arrived in February and a further four in December. Number 235 was part of the December delivery and is seen in Lord Street, Huddersfield, awaiting departure on service 64 to Bradford via Brighouse in October 1961. The service had been jointly operated with Bradford and Huddersfield JOC since 1929. *Travelens/Vic Nutton*

The Salford trade plate fastened to the radiator gives away that Willowbrook-bodied Leyland PS2 fleet number 42 had just been sold. It is pictured in the filling station close to the Blackfriars Street, Salford, offices of dealer Frank Cowley – a major player in the second hand bus market at the time. There were six vehicles in this much renumbered batch delivered in 1950 with dual-purpose seating and painted in the mostly cream coach livery. Originally 38-43, they became 16-21 in the fleet renumbering of June 1957, by late 1958 they had been downgraded to bus seating, renumbered 181-186 and painted in the livery shown in this 1962 picture. In 1960 they were changed again to 130-135. *Geoffrey Morant*

Hebble was an early convert to underfloor-engined single-deck vehicles, the first Leyland Royal Tigers arriving in 1951. These proved popular and the company returned to Leyland in 1953 for a further eight with Weymann bodywork, of which fleet number 164 (originally 64) is seen on the forecourt of Walnut Street Depot, Halifax, at Whitsuntide in 1966. *Linden Edwards*

In summer 1966, 30ft-long Weymann-bodied AEC Regent V 302 is pictured in Great Albion Street, Halifax, outside Crossfield Bus Station. Delivered in 1957, there were three in the batch; they were the first new vehicles with highbridge bodywork and were numbered 301-303 in a new 'highbridge' series. All Hebble's future double-deckers would be highbridge. *Linden Edwards*

Double-deck deliveries in 1958 were two 30ft-long forward-entrance Weymann-bodied AEC Regent V (304/05). This picture is of year-old 305 in Bradford in summer 1959 by which time sister vehicle 304 had met with an accident, overturning on North Bridge, Halifax, in May 1958. It was returned to Weymann to be rebuilt and re-entered service in August 1958 renumbered 306. Until 1960, these two, together with the similar 301-303 and 307-310, had cream-painted radiator cowl surrounds to indicate to drivers that they could not enter part of the Walnut Street depot due to height restrictions. *Geoffrey Morant*

After the batches of Leylands, Hebble turned to AEC for single-deckers. 189 was one of five Reliances with Willowbrook bodies delivered in 1959. It was photographed in August 1966 in Chester Street bus station, Bradford, with Ledgard vehicles to the right and a Yorkshire Woollen vehicle in cream on the X12 service to Manchester just visible on the left. *Linden Edwards*

Hebble continued to purchase AEC vehicles and in 1962 received four shorter AEC Regent Vs with the smaller AV470 engine. On Sunday 28th February 1971, the fleet by then renumbered into a common series with Yorkshire Woollen, 618 (new as 280) operated the final Hebble journey – the 23.10hrs departure from Bradford on route 17 to Halifax via Queensbury. The vehicle left Bradford with a full standing load, up the slow steep climb from Bradford to Queensbury, and then a speedier descent to Halifax. Thus ended the Hebble stage carriage operation which had begun in 1924. On the following day Hebble's fleet and operations passed to Halifax JOC and Yorkshire Woollen. *Peter Cain*

Pictured at Slack Top operating the basically hourly service between Burnley and Leeds, fleet number 134 was one of four AEC Reliances with Park Royal dual-purpose bodywork. In this summer 1965 view, the road surface has been removed for major work by one of the utility companies but traffic was expected to use the uneven surface. Although the service was timetabled from Burnley to Leeds, at Halifax passengers would to change to a different vehicle, usually a double-decker, for the onward journey to Leeds. *Linden Edwards*

Hebble purchased only one new rear-engined double-decker – this Daimler Fleetline with Northern Counties bodywork, delivered in April 1966. Prior to entering service, brand new 351 gleams in the sunshine in Gibbet Street, Halifax, opposite the Walnut Street depot. It might have been Hebble's only rear-engined bus but it was the first in full time service in Halifax, arriving a few months before the Corporation's seven almost identical vehicles – and in 1971 it would join them in the Halifax fleet. In 1969 a further Fleetline was transferred from Yorkshire Woollen, both passed to Yorkshire Woollen in March 1971 and thence to Calderdale JOC Halifax in August. *Linden Edwards*

Crossing North Bridge in Halifax – under which the former Great Northern Railway line from Halifax to Bradford or Keighley via Queensbury passed (and where Hebble AEC Regent 302 overturned) – in April 1970 is fleet number 287. It was one of fifteen Metro-Cammell bodied AEC Regent Vs that were new to Yorkshire Woollen in 1959. In 1969 as part of an area rationalisation, most of Yorkshire Woollen's services in the Halifax area and some vehicles passed to Hebble. This April 1970 picture shows it working former Yorkshire Woollen service 24 from Leeds; in the background the new Halifax inner relief road is under construction. Hebble's expansion did not last long – in a further reorganisation in March 1971 the stage services were transferred to Yorkshire Woollen or Halifax. *Linden Edwards*

Huddersfield

Huddersfield holds a proud place in the history of British municipal passenger transport; it was here in January 1883 that, by default, the first example of municipal operation of a tramway system began.

The Corporation's first motor bus route commenced in December 1920 from Paddock Head on the Dod Lea tram route to Golcar. More routes followed and eventually they were extended back into town with higher fares giving protection to the trams. Of the first 75 buses all but two were locally built Karriers. An agreement was reached with the LMS Railway Company in May 1930 for the sale of half the interest in the motorbus undertaking to the railway company; thus the Huddersfield Joint Omnibus Committee ('JOC') was formed; the corporation retaining the trams.

Corporation owned trolleybuses replaced the trams from 1933 onwards and the Corporation fleet strength (all trolleybuses) reached 140. Unlike the JOC buses the trolleys traversed the main thoroughfares on cross-town routes and were always held in high esteem by the travelling public possibly because of their lower fare structure and higher frequencies.

The JOC ran a mixed fleet of some 96 single- and double-deck buses with a preference for AEC and Daimler chassis. Low railway bridges saw the introduction of low bridge buses on the Holme Valley and Kirkheaton routes. One man operation was introduced in 1952 using two high capacity Guy Arab UFs on sparsely populated routes.

Trolleybus replacement on the West Vale route in November 1961 saw the start of a new series of Corporation-owned motorbuses which eventually totalled 104 – the new Leylands and Daimlers were painted in a streamlined livery to resemble the trolleybuses they replaced. Following more trolleybus replacements in 1966 some cross-town routes, known as coordinated services, were jointly operated by the Corporation and JOC.

Final takeover of the JOC took place by October 1969 – a government loan of £239,000 also enabled the Corporation to

both purchase Hanson's stage service operations and also the (by then) National Bus Company share of the JOC. This gave Huddersfield Corporation Passenger Transport Department a fleet of some 220 buses and an enlarged operating area. On the down side as part of the agreement its buses would no longer be seen in Dewsbury or on the recently acquired workings to Sheffield. Joint working however still continued to Bradford and Halifax. On 1st April 1974, as a result of local government reorganisation, the undertaking became part of the West Yorkshire Passenger Transport Executive.

This Saturday afternoon scene in the town's principal retail thoroughfare, John William Street, on 2 July 1966 illustrates the important role played by trolleybuses just two years before their end. In the lead is BUT/East Lancs 609 new 1953 followed by Sunbeam S7A/East Lancs 640 of 1959 – it was the last three-axle trolleybus built for British service. In the rear are Roe-bodied Leyland motorbuses which had replaced trolleybuses in earlier stages of the conversion programme.
Michael Russell

Huddersfield's post-war trolleybus replacement programme involved the purchase of 52 Sunbeam MS2 chassis, of which the first batch of 28 were badged as Karriers in accord with the undertaking's pre-war vehicle purchasing policy. Their Park Royal bodies had an unusual three-window layout at the upper deck front, with central outward-opening quarter-light – again continued from pre-war days. Many of their bodies were later replaced by new East Lancs or Roe products, but 542, shown here in September 1963, was one that retained its original until withdrawal in 1964. It is passing through St George's Square bound for Birkby on route 60, though incorrectly showing Crosland Hill. *Roy Marshall*

The majority of Huddersfield's initial trolleybus fleet ordered for the tramway replacement programme in the period 1933-1940, had Karrier E6 chassis. During the 17-year managership of Harold Muscroft, 28 were refurbished and then rebodied by Roe – the high standard of the undertaking's mechanical renovation work resulted in praise from the bodybuilders. Shown here, number 518 was originally Weymann-bodied and was rebodied in 1953, remaining in service until 1961 – some of the other pre-war Karriers lasted until conversion of the interurban Marsden route in January 1963. *Travelens/Vic Nutton*

Seen in October 1961, fleet number 79 was one of twelve Willowbrook-bodied Daimler CVG6s purchased in 1948 by the Joint Omnibus Committee (JOC); legal ownership, as normal was six each by both the Corporation and British Railways. They replaced older pre-war Regals and by 1950 the class totalled thirty. The East side of Byram Street in front of the GPO sorting office was the terminus for buses to Dalton, Kirkheaton, Upperheaton, and Nont Sarah's as well as to Cowcliffe. The crew of 79 are not in evidence – with an hourly frequency on the service they enjoyed a very lengthy layover. This vehicle was withdrawn in 1963 and a year later all thirty had been replaced. *Travelens/Vic Nutton*

Prior to 1949 the only lowbridge buses in the JOC fleet capable of safely negotiating the low railway bridges at Kirkheaton station and on Woodhead Road were the utility Daimlers. However in 1949 a batch of six AEC Regent IIIs with Northern Coach Builders bodies joined the fleet increasing the total of lowbridge buses to twenty five. Six pre-war highbridge Regents were withdrawn at the same time – general manager Harold Muscroft preferred the greater flexibility offered by the lowbridge replacements. Passengers on the longer Holme Valley routes who had suffered the upper-deck wooden slat seats of the utility vehicles no doubt appreciated the comfort of the new upholstered seating. By 1964 225 had been sold by the JOC to the Corporation and converted into a driver training vehicle numbered A11 in the service vehicle fleet. At this time large numbers of former trolleybus drivers were being trained to drive the replacement diesels. *Omnibus Society/Peter Henson*

When the Dod-Lea via Longwood tram route was replaced by trolleybuses in 1939, difficulty was encountered in finding a suitable turning facility. The settlement of Longwood is precipitously perched on a south-facing escarpment and the solution was to install a turntable mounted on concrete pillars projecting into a field. Its operation soon proved problematical given prevailing strong Pennine winds and the later wartime blackout conditions and in 1941 a simple triangular reverser was provided and the turntable locked. In early afternoon on 21 April 1965, trolleybus 598 is seen reversing onto the platform. This Sunbeam MS2 with 70-seat Roe bodywork was new in 1951 and withdrawn in 1966. *Michael Russell*

Seen from the field below, the concrete pillars supporting the turntable platform are clearly visible, together with the traction poles of extraordinary length that carried the end strains of the overhead wiring. A serious accident, fortunately without personal injury, took place here in February 1967 when, during careless reversing, trolleybus 634 punctured the protective guard railings, fell into the field below and was written off. The trolleybus shown in this view, dating from 17 June 1967, is BUT/East Lancs number 627, new in 1956. *Michael Russell*

East Lancs-bodied AEC Regent III 172 was one of a batch of six purchased in 1951 for the JOC. It is pictured in November 1969 in Upperhead Row bus station laying over after a peak hour duty shortly after the JOC passed into transport history. Double deckers had been used on the Colne Valley services since 1959 but the front and side via destination displays are incompatible as the bus can not have returned from Scapegoat Hill via both Leymoor and Scar Lane. *Geoffrey Morant*

In the years 1952 to 1955 the JOC took delivery of eighteen AEC Regent IIIs with East Lancs lowbridge bodywork. New in 1954 number 232 is seen in November 1969 by then owned by Huddersfield Corporation Passenger Transport Department. A month after the Hanson bus business was acquired, 232 is travelling down South Parade towards Chapel Hill on the former Hanson service to Meltham via Milnsbridge and Helme. It was not yet equipped with blinds to show the correct new route number 90 or the intermediate points. The displayed number 2 did however imply that the bus would travel via Manchester Road and Milnsbridge and not via Netherton on the old JOC route. *Geoffrey Morant*

A quiet scene in the Upperhead Row bus station with178, one of six East Lancs-bodied AEC Regent IIIs of 1955, not yet ready to depart for Hill Top on the Colne Valley Service jointly operated with Hanson. Joseph Hanson had first reached Hill Top by an extension of his Slaithwaite Service via Crimble Bank in January 1928. A year later Hanson entered into a pooling arrangement with the Corporation as a means of obtaining the necessary licences for all his services. A further agreement in September 1939 saw the Hill Top route become part of the jointly operated Colne Valley Services. Some journeys were extended further up the valley to the hamlet of Wilberlee overlooked by the Moorside Edge radio transmitter. *Don Akrigg*

Replacing a similar number of pre-war Regals a further batch of five Guy Arab UFs with Guy-Park Royal bodies were purchased for the JOC in 1954. The stock of seven Guy UFs enabled the whole of services 35/36 (Marsden/Slaithwaite via Scholes), 25 (Inner Circle), 18 (Thurstonland/ Stocksmoor) and 55 (Nont Sarah's) to be one-man operated. Shown in the mid 1960s adjacent to the new Civic Centre in High Street the bus has just returned from Wood Nook. This route was started in 1930 by Holmfirth independent Wilson Haigh and passed to the JOC in 1934. It was useful for shift workers living in Honley, who could walk from the terminus to the David Brown factories at Meltham Mills. *Linden Edwards*

Following the demolition of the West side of Buxton Road inward bound buses were diverted from Chapel Hill via South Parade where fully-laden Roe-bodied AEC Reliance 9 is seen passing the new Police Headquarters building with the old clock tower of the Cooperative building in the background. One of five purchased in 1956 for the JOC the bus is pictured in 1972 working for the now enlarged Huddersfield Corporation Passenger Transport Department. Showing a white blank in the route number box it has possibly operated a peak-hour short working on the 35/36 from Meltham or Holmfirth. *Roy Marshall*

One of six East Lancs bodied AEC Reliances delivered early in 1959, increasing the number of pay as you enter buses in the JOC fleet to 18. This allowed new general manager Edgar Dyson to extend one man operation to further routes including Wood Nook, Blackmoorfoot, Lepton and Cowcliffe. Pictured in October 1969 in Upperhead Row bus station, number 13 is ready to depart for Blackmoorfoot on one of only eight weekday round trips. This was a relatively new route only started in 1948 as part of the joint Colne Valley Services; at first all the mileage was operated by Hanson which had a small bus suitable for one man operation. *Roy Marshall*

For evaluation purposes a pair of Guy Arab IV buses with East Lancs bodywork and the newly introduced Gardner 6LX engine entered service in 1959 for the JOC. Some eight years later the second of the two, 191, stands out of service with its cab windscreen shattered. The crew stand on the pavement, awaiting help. *Omnibus Society/Peter Henson*

The junction at Longroyd Bridge on 16 June 1967, with BUT/East Lancs 627, new 1956, turning from Manchester Road into Longroyd Lane working a journey on route 41 to Paddock – a regular short-working service on the Longwood route. Longroyd Bridge depot is behind and to the right of the camera and the overhead wiring in the foreground is a depot-connection curve. Behind is Daimler CVG6/Roe motorbus 426, new in 1964, operating on route 51, a replacement for the former Marsden trolleybus route closed in January 1963. The Daimler was one of a batch of 16 (425-440) bought for February 1964 conversion of the Crosland Hill route (60), which branched off from the Marsden route a few hundred yards further south on Manchester Road. *Michael Russell*

It was said that the inscription 'Huddersfield' on the entablature of the town's magnificent railway station, opened in 1847, was superfluous as the building could be nowhere else. During most of the post-war period, northbound trolleybuses on the Bradley, Birkby and Fixby (originally Brighouse) routes passed in front of the portico but by the time that this view was taken on 16 June 1967, the wiring in St George's Square was reduced to use by vehicles terminating in the town centre or returning to the depot from Lindley or Outlane. At the end of the morning peak period, Sunbeam S7A/East Lancs 636 of 1959 and BUT 9641T/East Lancs 617 of 1953 are shown en route to Longroyd Bridge depot after working special journeys for pupils at Salendine Nook schools. *Michael Russell*

Features of the Huddersfield trolleybus system which were apparent to any observer were the immaculate condition in which the fleet was traditionally turned out, free of external advertisements, that all the vehicles were three-axle and that the routes passed through spectacular, rugged Pennine scenery. A fine example was Quarmby Clough on the Longwood route, where BUT/East Lancs no. 617, dating from 1953, is seen on 15 June 1967 on Vicarage Road, heading for the horseshoe bend that will take it into Longwood village. This was Huddersfield's penultimate trolleybus route, converted to motorbus operation in the following month. *Michael Russell*

In this March 1969 picture fleet number 194, one of a pair of East Lancs bodied AEC Regent Vs new in 1961, waits on the West side of Lord Street for the 1.45pm departure to Rawthorpe against a background of leafless trees in St Peter's gardens and the Victorian buildings in Byram Street. They were the JOC's first 30 feet long double deckers. *Roy Marshall*

The JOC's first and only Leyland double deckers were six Roe-bodied Leyland PD2A/24s delivered in 1963 and a new numbering sequence (101-106) was started for them. They were shorter versions of the 70-seater Corporation owned PD3A/2s. Seen here in 1967 on the East side of Byram Street 103 was able to work on the Kirkheaton service following the demolition of the low railway bridge one year earlier. When new these Titans often operated joint Golcar circulars as Hanson also used 65-seater double-deckers. *Geoffrey Morant*

Huddersfield Corporation purchased its first batch of eight trolleybus-replacement motor buses in 1961. The Roe-bodied Leyland PD3As were painted in 'streamlined' red and cream livery similar to that of the trolleybuses. A new numbering sequence started at 401 and the second member of the batch, 402, is seen here in April 1963 at the Dalton Black Horse terminus before completion of a new turning circle. It had originally been intended to extend the 72 trolleybus route from Moldgreen via Long Lane but instead from November 1962 a new motor bus-operated cross-town service was introduced from Crosland Road to Dalton, Black Horse. The destination Town Centre on the blind possibly signifies the end of a peak period after which only two of the three buses would be required for the reduced 30-minute frequency. *Roy Marshall*

Loading in Holmfirth under the watchful eye of an inspector on a cold February day in 1971, Roe-bodied AEC Reliance 23 was one of a pair new to the JOC in 1963. Following their arrival in the fleet the last two crew-operated Daimler single-deckers were withdrawn. The 18-mile route 35 from Marsden to Huddersfield via Meltham, Holmfirth, Scholes and New Mill was Huddersfield's longest – but was so circuitous that only enthusiasts or someone wanting to enjoy the Pennine scenery on a pleasant afternoon drive was likely to travel the full distance. To the staff the route, along with the 36 variant to Slaithwaite, was known as 'Over the Tops' as it linked the Colne and Holme Valleys. *Linden Edwards*

Parked in St George's Square, 114 is one of a batch of four Roe-bodied Daimler CVG6LXs new to the JOC in 1964. It is pictured here after April 1967 with the blinds set for one of the 'coordinated services' introduced at that time following an agreement between the Corporation and the JOC to reduce the annual overall mileage with a considerable projected annual cost saving. Cross Town route 23 was an amalgamation of the former JOC route to Meltham and the Corporation route to Riddings. *Linden Edwards*

Pictured in front of the Commercial Hotel in New Street, fleet number 446 is about to turn right into High Street on its cross Town route from Birkby to Balmoral Avenue, Crosland Moor. New to the Corporation in 1965 it was one of a batch of sixteen Roe-bodied Daimler CVG6LXs; by the time this picture was taken in April 1974 it had been repainted in the chosen version of several experimental liveries introduced after the amalgamation of the former Corporation, Hanson and JOC fleets. *Roy Marshall*

A change in Corporation vehicle policy saw the entry into service in July 1967 of sixteen Daimler Fleetlines with, as usual, Roe bodies. Although suitable for driver-only operation initially they were two-man operated. Shown here in 1972 negotiating the Chapel Hill roundabout in front of the Albion public house 487 is about to turn right into Manchester Road on the former trolleybus route from Bradley to Longwood. *Geoffrey Morant*

A pair of Leyland Leopards with bodies by East Lancs-associated Neepsend entered service for the JOC in 1967 replacing the original pioneering pay-as-you-enter Guys 1-2. The bodies of 25/26 were the first one-man single-deckers in the fleet not to feature an enclosed drivers' cab with offside door – the driver now entered by the passenger door. Pictured here when six years-old 26 is unloading at a temporary stand on the former coach parking area. In the background the almost complete new multi-storey car park and bus station can be seen with the much older Plumbers Arms public house on the extreme right in Macaulay Street. *Roy Marshall*

Two of these Roe-bodied AEC Swifts joined the JOC fleet late in 1967. They were Huddersfield's first rear engined single deckers and at 33 feet, the longest vehicles then in the fleet, but were also the last AECs to be purchased by the JOC. In March 1968, three months old number 28 awaits departure on the joint Colne Valley service to Slaithwaite via Manchester Road and Scar Lane. The glass fronted new Civic Centre complete with Corporation crest forms the background and the timetable frame can be seen in the shelter in this Top Bus Station view. *Linden Edwards*

The final batch of buses delivered to the JOC entered service in March 1969 and were six Roe bodied Daimler Fleetlines, which allowed the disposal of the last six surviving lowbridge buses. Fitted ready for one-man operation they were equipped with periscopes to allow the driver to observe the upper deck. Pictured in April 1972 at one of the temporary shelters erected after demolition of the original Top Bus Station 125 is seen loading for the circular service to Golcar running outwards via Manchester Road and returning via Paddock Head. The unusual circular structure in the left background is the top of the ventilation shaft from Springwood railway tunnel. *Geoffrey Morant*

The first new buses delivered to the enlarged Corporation undertaking were nine 33ft-long Seddon RUs with Gardner 6HLX engines and Pennine Coachcraft (Seddon) bodies with front entrance and centre exit. Seen in July 1970 leaving The Bottom (or Manchester Street) Bus Station via the Granby Street exit, fleet number 34 is working the circular service to Beaumont Park outwards via Woodside Road and inwards via Walpole Road. In the background the inspector's hut, used by conductors for paying in and the George and Dragon public house have yet to be demolished. *Linden Edwards*

The 1971 batch of six Roe-bodied Daimler Fleetlines were the first dual-door double-deckers to enter the fleet. Photographed at 'Rushworths Corner' – the junction of John William Street and Westgate – 134 was heading for the Meltham loading point then located in the Market Place. This was the first cross-town route served by one-man double-deckers; the route itself was formed by linking the former Hanson Meltham via Helme route with the JOC's Bradley circular. *Geoffrey Morant*

Ledgard

SAMUEL LEDGARD

Samuel Ledgard's entry to the field of transport started with steam wagons for his outside catering business. From 1896 until his death in 1952 he was the landlord of the Nelson Hotel, which was adjacent to his garage at Armley Road, Armley in Leeds. Other activities included brewing, haulage and quarrying and the haulage fleet was increased in January 1940 when Otley Carriers Limited was purchased whilst his quarrying interests included owning Lingerfield Sand and Gravel Company.

A Karrier lorry, U 1949, was purchased in 1912 and in 1913 having been fitted with an interchangeable coach body it was used for weekly services to Scarborough and Blackpool along with two others, a Karrier and a Dennis. After the 1914-1918 war four new and four reconditioned Caledons were fitted with interchangeable bodies. At the time Ledgard was the agent for the make. Summer 1920 saw the resumption of the Scarborough and Blackpool services.

Stage carriage services started in 1924 when Ledgard joined forces with J Cole and Sons Limited and G F Tate Limited in the operation of the Leeds to Otley via Bramhope route. Later in 1924 the business of Ward, Horsforth was acquired which brought the Horsforth to Leeds via Hawksworth Road route to Ledgard. Further acquisitions were the Cream Bus Service of Burley-in-Wharfedale in 1925, Jules Antichan of Burley-in-Wharfedale in 1927 and Barrett and Thornton of Otley also in 1927. In 1932 the Moorfield Bus Company of Yeadon was acquired and in 1935 the business of B and B Tours Limited of Bradford was purchased. This had been formed in July 1928 by the two directors of Blythe & Berwick (1928) Limited after their stage carriage service had passed to West Yorkshire. This purchase gave Ledgard a Bradford to Blackpool express service and the Bradford to Harrogate service via Menston and Otley.

The pre-war fleet additions were mainly Leylands with Leyland-bodied Titans and Duple-

Park Place in Leeds was used by Ledgard's buses as a layover area to avoid congestion on the departure stands. AEC Regent V NCY 455 with a Weymann body, one of four acquired from South Wales and which entered service in 1967 is arriving from Horsforth on the service via Hawksworth Road whilst ex-London AEC Regent III MXX 147 has arrived on the service from Bradford via Pudsey. Both will move forward to King Street as their departure times approach.
Roy Marshall

PNW 92 was the middle one of three all-Leyland PD2s which were new in 1952 and were the last buses purchased before Samuel Ledgard's death. They were delivered in grey primer since Samuel had worked out that he could paint them for £165 each compared to the £250 which Leyland had quoted. Seen here in Chester Street Bus Station in Bradford it is working the service to Leeds via Pudsey, with West Yorkshire buses in the other half of this divided bus station. *Photobus*

bodied Tigers although, in addition to the many and varied vehicles acquired with the various businesses, new Guy, Karrier, ADC, Chevrolet, Dennis, Maudslay, Albion and Daimler models appeared in the fleet between 1924 and 1935.

Wartime saw the usual deliveries of two Guy Arabs followed by fourteen utility Daimlers and also four Bedford OWBs. Deliveries of Leylands resumed in 1946 with six Leyland-bodied PD1s followed by eight Duple-bodied PS1s for the coach fleet in 1948. Leylands, in the form of six PD2s, followed for the bus fleet until 1952 whilst the coach fleet received seven Plaxton-bodied Fodens.

Samuel Ledgard's death on April 4th 1952 was a major blow. The death duties were extensive and after the many bequests which he had left in his will to members of his staff for their loyal service over the years there was little money left for the executors to continue running the business in the same manner as before. Their solution was to purchase second-hand buses when replacements were needed. However they felt that this was inappropriate for coaches and in order to purchase new ones in 1955 they sold three of the sand and gravel companies then known as Samuel Ledgard (Quarries) Ltd. In the same year the small haulage company, S Ledgard (Carriers) Ltd based in Otley was also sold enabling them to concentrate on the bus fleet.

Whilst many of the buses and coaches withdrawn during his lifetime were sold quickly, a great number were parked on the roof of the garage at Armley. These were sold, after his death to G.W. Butler (dealer) for scrap and included Karriers new in 1913 and 1914 which had been withdrawn in 1921 and 1927 and two Caledons from 1916 and 1919 also withdrawn in 1927. More than thirty buses and coaches were on the roof at Armley and disposed of in this way whilst others were disposed of from Otley to the same dealer.

After Samuel Ledgard's death the Executors purchased large numbers of second-hand vehicles for both the bus and the coach fleets, the only new ones being six Burlingham-bodied coaches in 1955 and the six AEC Regent Vs and a Daimler CVG6 in 1957. From 1964 to 1967 new coaches were hired from Stanley Hughes, the Gomersal dealer. In total 142 second hand buses and coaches entered service with Ledgard between 1953 and 1967. The last business to be acquired was that of J W Kitchin, Pudsey in April 1957 with four buses and the route from Troydale, on the outskirts of Pudsey, to Calverley.

There were garages (shown with their October 1967 vehicle allocation) at Armley (60), Bradford (11), Yeadon (10), Otley (24) and Ilkley (Outstation of Otley – no permanent allocation). The business was sold to the West Yorkshire Road Car Co in October 1967 and although the fleet of almost one hundred passed to West Yorkshire only fourteen were taken into stock. Three of the routes were sold by West Yorkshire to Leeds City Transport – Leeds to Bradford via Pudsey (jointly with Bradford) and the Leeds to Horsforth via Hawksworth Road and the Pudsey to Calverley service which had been acquired with the Kitchin business.

After Samuel Ledgard's death in 1952 the Executors purchased a large quantity of second-hand buses starting with fourteen Daimler CWA6s from London Transport in 1953. The parking triangle outside the Drill Hall was conveniently close to Otley Bus Station and here HGF 891 with a Park Royal body, one of a further ten acquired in 1954, is seen resplendent in a new coat of paint. *Roy Marshall*

Following the acquisition of the ex-London Daimlers in 1953/4 a further five Daimler CWA6s, new in 1943/4, were acquired from Midland Red in 1957. One had a Weymann body, the others being Duple bodied and all had been rebuilt by Willowbrook in 1950/1. GHA 965 is one of the Duple-bodied ones and is seen in Otley Bus Station on the local Weston Estate service. They lasted only a short while with Ledgard, all having been withdrawn by 1961. *Ken Jubb*

When Leeds City Transport withdrew its ten Brush-bodied Daimler CVD6s they were all acquired by Ledgard in 1960 and LNW 530, the penultimate one, is seen in Commercial Road, Kirkstall having just crossed the junction with Kirkstall Hill and Bridge Road whilst operating the service from Horsforth, the same terminus to which Leeds had operated them but via a different route. There was much adverse comment in the local press at the time from the citizens of Leeds about the wasteful sale but they were non-standard in the Leeds fleet. *Donald Wilson*

Opposite page Passing the Fairway Hotel in Foundry Approach, Leeds, in September 1959 is Ledgard's HGF 948 – a Daimler CWA6 which originated with London Transport in October 1946 with a Park Royal highbridge body. It was one of twenty-three such buses purchased by Ledgard in 1953/54 and whilst the remainder entered service with their double-deck bodies, HGF 948 was rebodied using the Brush centre entrance coach body new in 1935 on Ledgard's Maudslay SF40 registered CUB 1 which had been withdrawn in 1951; the body being rebuilt locally by Rhodes to suit the Daimler chassis. It ran in this form from April 1954 until withdrawn in January 1960 following a serious accident. *John Kaye*

One of four buses acquired with the stage service of J W Kitchin of Pudsey in 1957, this 1951 Guy-bodied Guy Arab UF was the second bus to carry the registration GUY 3 as a Guy demonstrator and was fitted with a pre-selector gearbox with a floor mounted selector control unit when new – replaced in 1964 with a standard column-mounted unit. Seen leaving Otley Bus Station with a full load it is on the service to Horsforth. The previous GUY 3 was a Guy Arab III demonstrator, later re-registered JJW 239, and was another of the four buses acquired from Kitchin, the other two being Burlingham-bodied Atkinson PL745Hs. *Geoffrey Morant*

In 1959 five Bristol K6As, which had been new in 1945, were acquired from United Automobile Services and the second of them, GHN 635, is seen on a somewhat dreary day in Otley Bus Station on the Horsforth service. When new they had Strachan lowbridge bodies and these had been replaced in 1954/55 with second hand Eastern Coachworks bodies, new in 1949, which had been removed from even older United vehicles which themselves had been rebodied. *John May*

76

The last new buses for Ledgard were six Roe-bodied AEC Regent Vs delivered in 1962 as 1949 U – 1954 U. Ledgard's first bus in 1912 had been a Karrier, U 1949, hence the choice of registration numbers for this batch. The green roof was the standard treatment for many years and derived from the first double-deckers delivered in 1930 – Leyland-bodied Leyland TD1s which had wooden-panelled roofs covered in green waterproof canvas. Samuel Ledgard liked this and so subsequent double-deckers had the roof painted green. 1952 U is seen loading in King Street, Leeds, for the service to Ilkley via Guiseley with a Hebble Willowbrook bodied Leyland Royal Tiger on the Rochdale service and another Ledgard bus on the Bradford service stand. *John Kaye*

Pictured in August 1967 operating the Otley local service to the Weston Estate, BCK 633, a 1947 Samlesbury (Leyland sub contract) -bodied Leyland PD1 acquired from Preston Corporation is passing the bus station in Otley. It was one of seven Preston buses acquired in 1961 along with four Leylands from Ribble and five from the Bristol Omnibus Company at the same time. *Roy Marshall*

A busy scene in Chester Street Bus Station in Bradford with Ledgard's LAE 2, a 1948 BBW-bodied Leyland PD1 acquired from Bristol in 1960 on the Leeds via Fartown service and being followed by MLL 828, an ex-London RT on the Leeds via Pudsey service. *John May*

One of four Leyland RTL class buses acquired from London Transport in 1966, LLU 853 is seen in Robin Lane, Pudsey in August 1967 on the service from Leeds to Bradford. It appears that the climb up Lowtown, the turning in the right background, has proved a little too much on this occasion with the driver waiting for a relief bus to arrive to replace the overheating Leyland. *Alan Mortimer*

Making the turn into Otley Bus Station is one of four ex-London Transport RLH class Weymann-bodied AEC Regent IIIs new in 1950 which were acquired by Ledgard in 1964 and 1965. Photographed in August 1967, KYY 502 is on the service to Horsforth. In the background is West Yorkshire Bristol Lodekka DX36. *Roy Marshall*

Having travelled down Low Side on its journey from Horsforth, MXX 149, ex-London Transport, is leaning over as it rounds the bend into Hawksworth Road on its way to Leeds. It is one of twenty-three AEC RT type Regent IIIs acquired from London Transport in 1963. A further sixteen were acquired in 1964 and 1965. The destination blinds showed the incorrect Hawkesworth Road. August 1967. *Alan Mortimer*

This AEC Regent III, dating from 1948, with bodywork by Roberts of Horbury, Wakefield – a firm more usually associated with railway carriage and wagon construction – had been acquired from its original owner Felix of Hatfield in January 1962 along with a Leyland bodied PD2. GWY 157 is seen outside the Moorfield Garage at Yeadon a little over two weeks before Ledgard ceased operations. *Nicholas Harris*

Waiting in Otley Bus Station, on a typically wet day, to depart on the service to Horsforth via White Cross route is DRN 273, a Leyland-bodied Leyland PD2, one of four acquired from Ribble Motor Services in 1964. *John May*

Ledgard acquired two 1954 AEC Regent IIIs with Weymann bodies from Devon General in 1966 and PDV 726 is seen in Chester Street Bus Station, Bradford loading for the service via Pudsey to Leeds. The car on the right is parked in Chester Street which divided the bus station in two, the other half being used by West Yorkshire and also by Ledgard's service to Harrogate via Otley. *Peter Roberts*

In April 1960 Ledgard purchased this Daimler demonstrator SDU 711, a CVG6 with a Willowbrook body which at 14 feet high was some six inches lower than conventional highbridge buses – achieved by the construction of the body directly onto the chassis ('semi integral') – Daimler had modified the chassis lowering the gearbox and modifying the rear axle casing. It was one of only twelve of Ledgard's buses to enter service with West Yorkshire after the takeover and is seen here repainted by its new owner and numbered DGW11 – but still working a former Ledgard service. *Nicholas Harris*

In December 1966/January 1967 Ledgard placed in service four AEC Regent Vs with Weymann bodies acquired from the South Wales Transport Co Ltd. Emerging from the parking yard behind Otley Garage is NCY 453, the last of the four to enter service. All four passed to West Yorkshire as DAW1-4 in October 1967 and NCY 453 is seen here carrying its new West Yorkshire fleet number DAW3 on the bonnet surround and also the West Yorkshire fleetname. *Nicholas Harris*

Leeds

In 1946 the bus fleet in Leeds was relatively small with 278 buses compared to 432 trams. With the tram replacement programme this changed gradually until, in the last year of the trams – 1959, there were 631 buses and 110 trams. The final size of the Leeds bus fleet in 1974 was 702, a mixture of single and double deck types.

Postwar, Leeds had a multiple sourcing policy for chassis and bodies – AEC, Leyland and Daimler for chassis and Roe or the MCW group for bodies, although AEC and Roe, the latter based in the city, tended to be favoured. There were separate series of fleet numbers, allocated in blocks of 100, for each make of chassis.

Two unusual features of the Leeds fleet for a number of years appeared on the front dash panel of some of the double-deckers. A number from 1 to 8 in white indicated the height group for the setting of the bus washer whilst a white 'H' on a small red plate indicated that the bus was fitted with a heater in the cooling system for overnight outside parking where suitable connecting sockets were provided. In addition fog lights and adjustable radiator blinds were normally fitted to exposed radiator buses on 1st October each year and removed on 1st April. Another Leeds feature, which stood out against the fleet's dark green livery, was the polished metal bonnet, left unpainted and easy to clean off oily finger marks.

After the war and until 1950 the livery had been blue and cream for trams and two shades of blue for the buses but a decision was made to change the trams to red and cream and the buses to two shades of green after several experimental liveries were tried including red and green for the trams and green and red for the buses.

It was normal for a Leeds bus to be exhibited on the Roe stand at the Commercial Motor Shows and this was an AEC Regent from 1935 until 1956 with a Leyland PD3 at the 1958 show and whilst there was no vehicle at the 1960 show subsequent exhibits were AEC Reliance, Daimler Fleetline, AEC Swift and Leyland Atlantean models with one of the Mercedes-Benz minibuses also at the 1970 show.

A representative sample of the Leeds fleet in the layover area of the Central Bus Station in September 1966 with AEC Regent III 601, AEC Regent V 857, Daimler Fleetline 121 and Leyland PD3 272. All had bodywork built by Roe at its Crossgates Carriage Works in the east of the City. They all have the small white signs (on the front edge of the canopy on the half cabs) which when illuminated displayed 'LIMITED' – on services where there was an alternative service over part of the route, there were restrictions on setting down passengers on outward journeys on Monday to Friday evening peak hour service and Saturday lunch times and the sign would be illuminated to show this. The vehicles have the modified destination layout with a route number replacing the earlier arrangement which normally had two or sometimes three via points in addition to the route number. *Don Akrigg*

Fifteen of these Leyland PD1s, 319-333, with Roe bodies formed the first batch of post-war buses delivered to Leeds in April/May 1946. They spent most of their working days from Bramley Garage after it was converted from a tram depot in January 1949, normally working the 46 service from Bramley to Belle Isle and Middleton. Number 322 is seen here in September 1959 in Butt Lane, Farnley, on a special tour shortly before withdrawal. *John Kaye*

The order for fifty Roe bodied AEC Regent IIIs, 401-450, was modified to include one using Park Royal metal framing which became 450, delivered in July 1949 a year after the Roe bodied ones. No more were delivered and Leeds continued to take composite bodies from Roe. Infirmary Street, leading from City Square, with the Post Office building behind was the loading point for this service 29 to Middleton, a housing estate in the southern suburbs and also for the service 72 to Bradford, operated jointly with Bradford City Transport. *Travelens/Vic Nutton*

After one early post-war Crossley-bodied Crossley DD42, 27, had been delivered in July 1946, Leeds took delivery of twenty more in late 1948/early 1949 by which time number 27 had been renumbered 701. Numbered 702-721 they spent a large part of their lives on the services from the Central Bus Station to Dib Lane (67), Foundry Lane (68) and Seacroft (78/79) in the eastern suburbs. In September 1959 708 is seen at the Foundry Lane terminus about to return to the Central Bus Station. *John Kaye*

Opposite top Following deliveries of Daimlers and Crossleys Leeds continued its policy of buying Roe-bodied AECs and passing the Central Bus Station en route from Torre Road Garage In August 1962 is 469, one of twenty-five Roe 'Pullman' bodied AEC Regent IIIs, numbered 451-475, from 1949. A notable feature of Leeds' fleet was the polished engine cover making it easy to remove oil and grease marks. *Alan Mortimer*

Opposite bottom Delivered in 1949–1950 Leyland PD2s with Leyland bodies 340-399 were largely allocated to the newly opened Bramley Garage which initially operated services to the west of the city and later, with tramway replacement, ran cross-city services such as the 11 from Gipton to Swinnow as seen here with 344 just about to pass the Central Bus Station In August 1962. These were the last buses to enter service without the 'Limited' signs, which were later added under the canopy and on the platform. Alan Mortimer

Whilst the majority of Leeds' post-war body orders were placed locally with Roe, from 1952 onwards there was a return to a pre-war pattern of buying a small number of bodies in most years from either Metro Cammell or Weymann. The first six post-war ones were AEC Regents 649 to 654, delivered in 1952 with Weymann bodies. This view, taken at the terminus of service 7 in Queenswood Drive, Headingley, shows another feature of the Leeds fleet – radiator shield and fog light normally fitted to Leeds buses between October and April each year. *Nicholas Harris*

Roe-bodied PD2s 301-310 were PD2/14s with preselector gearboxes and, apart from one other (at Walsall). Unique outside London, they could confuse drivers, as John Kaye recalled: 'Based at Torre Road garage they operated mainly on the 69/70 routes and, downhill, with a following wind, you might get 29 mph out of them. In my last summer conducting job they had been transferred to Bramley garage which had the PD1s and the PD2/1s, which could readily exceed 40mph. Allocated a PD2/14 for a Night Service I protested to the foreman. He grinned and suggested I stick with it. I soon found out when, going down Stanningley Road, we overtook the Bradford Corporation bus – something unheard of. The Bramley mechanics had done their usual to the fuel pump and the governor and 301-310 performed as well as the PD2/1s. The transmission did, however, catch out the drivers. I was on one when the driver preselected second ready for the next stop. The stop wasn't needed so he accelerated and then pressed the change pedal – whereupon the gearbox went into second and the bus more or less stopped – but the passengers didn't. *May 1967 Linden Edwards*

Twenty Leyland PD2s were ordered to replace the tram service to Half Mile Lane and were the first production PD2s to have the two-pedal control 'Pneumocyclic' gearbox. Entering service in 1955 201-215 were bodied by Roe and the last five, 216-220 by Metro-Cammell. In this August 1969 picture 220 is arriving at the Central Bus Station at the end of its journey from Pudsey via Half Mile Lane. The 'staircase' window was unique to those Leeds Orions which were fitted with the Roe patent safety staircase, which had a halfway landing. *John Kaye*

Continuing its policy of dual sourcing bodywork the 1954 AEC Regent IIIs, 730-759, included five with Metro-Cammell bodies, the remaining twenty-five being bodied by Roe. Metro-Cammell bodied 755 is turning from St Peter's Street into the Central Bus Station on its journey from Ireland Wood, a housing estate in the northern suburbs, the building in the background being Quarry Hill flats constructed in 1938 and housing 938 families at the time it was the largest social housing complex in the United Kingdom. *Geoffrey Morant*

Leeds required a small number of single deck vehicles because of two routes which crossed a bridge with a weight restriction, one also passing under a low bridge in Bramley. When the time came to replace the Leyland TS8s, Leeds chose to order eight buses with standee-type centre-entrance bodies from Roe. Three Leyland Tiger Cubs 29-31, two Guy Arab LUFs 35-36 and three AEC Reliances 32-34 were new in 1954/5. All had manual transmission which was unusual for Leeds and the drivers had full-width cabs. They all had the gold lining normally applied only to Leeds vehicles exhibited at the Commercial Motor Show. In June 1960 AEC Reliance 32 crosses the river Aire at Bridge Road Kirkstall before crossing the bridge over the Leeds & Liverpool canal which had the weight restriction. *Geoffrey Morant*

On its journey around the western suburbs from Harehills in the north east to Wortley in the south west of the city, Roe-bodied Guy Arab LUF 35 is about to turn left from Cockshott Lane to go down Stanningley Road in Bramley. *Roy Marshall*

Fleet number 562 was one of twenty Weymann-bodied Daimler CVG6, 552-571 delivered in 1957, following on from twenty (532-551) in 1956 which had similar looking Metro-Cammell bodies. The normal service to Elland Road was route 8 and the route number 102 displayed here indicates a Football Special service with special fares. These ran non-stop from the city centre to the Leeds United football ground. The location is South Parade and the date 14th November 1970. *Linden Edwards*

Two more standee single-deckers, 37/38, were bought in 1959 to replace the two Leyland PS1s dating from 1948. They were AEC Reliances but this time with semi-automatic transmission and again had Roe bodies with the area to the left of the driver not used for passenger accommodation. The first of the pair is seen in March 1967, after the Wortley to Harehills route round the western and northern suburbs of the city had been extended to Stanks in the north east of the city. *Geoffrey Morant*

A large fleet of AEC Regent Vs was built up from 1956 onwards, mainly for replacement of withdrawn tram services. The first were 760-839 in 1956 and these were followed by 840-894 in 1957, all with Roe bodies and 'normal' radiator cowls. The following fifteen, 895-909, delivered in mid-1958 were Leeds' first 8ft- wide double-deckers since Regent IIIs 626 to 648 in late 1950. Such a reversion from 8ft-wide to 7ft 6in was unusual. In St Peter's Street outside the Central Bus Station, 908 passes to the nearside of 906 which is waiting to enter the bus station. *Omnibus Society/ Peter Henson*

Leeds continued to prefer buses with exposed radiators and the last of these were fourteen AEC Regent Vs with Metro-Cammell bodies which were new in May 1960. The first, 910, is seen in New Market Street bound for Horsforth on cross city service 24. They were 30ft-long and, in line with Leeds' policy, had semi-automatic transmission – the last new double deckers with manual gearboxes were the Leyland PD2s of 1949/50. *Omnibus Society/Peter Henson*

An order originally intended to be eighty 27ft-long buses for tram replacement was changed to one for seventy-one 30ft-long ones, which gave an equivalent seating capacity. Leyland won the order with its PD3 chassis; their Roe bodies seated 39/32 but the seating was altered a year later to seat 38 in the upper-saloon after a new union agreement on standing passengers. Numbered 221-291 they were the first 30ft-long double-deck buses in the Leeds fleet and entered service in 1959. In this July 1970 scene 239 is on the cross-city service from Lower Wortley to Harehills on the revised city centre routeing from late 1968 as a result of road improvements removing the right turn from Eastgate to New York Road. *Roy Marshall*

Continuing to divide its orders between chassis makers Leeds placed further orders with Daimler and ten CVG6LX/30 were delivered in 1962 all with Roe bodies. Numbers 572-576 had front entrances and 577-581 the more normal, for Leeds, rear entrances. 578 from the latter group is seen passing the Central Bus Station on the cross-city service from Seacroft in the east to Whingate in the west in August 1962. Twenty similar rear-entrance Daimlers followed – 582-596 in 1963 and 111-115 in 1964.
Alan Mortimer

The five front-entrance Daimler CVG6LX/30s, 572-576, entered service in May 1962 principally on the Leeds – Bradford service 72, jointly operated with Bradford City Transport which was using front entrance AEC Regent Vs. Both operators then introduced rear engined buses to the route and, being non-standard, 572-576 were advertised for sale in 1966. Surprisingly they failed to find a buyer and continued in service, passing to the PTE. Here, its lower sides covered in road grime, number 573 is in the small yard at the rear of Bramley garage which had been converted from a tram depot at the beginning of 1949. *Linden Edwards*

Leyland's share of the 1962/63/64 deliveries were Weymann-bodied PD3s 311-320 (1962) and 321-330 (1963). This is 312, seen in New Market Street, on a journey from Roundhay in the north of the city to Middleton in the south. The route was part of the last but one group of tram services to be replaced by buses in March 1959.
Linden Edwards

A somewhat unusual use for city double-deckers was tours. In the 1950s and 1960s several municipalities began to run City Sightseeing Tours. Lasting a full afternoon they visited places of interest and beauty spots in the city and beyond. Leeds, Halifax and Huddersfield ran them – Halifax's, for example, took passengers to see the M62 construction sites, Scammonden Reservoir and the Pennines. Those of Leeds toured the city and then went out in the countryside, visiting the city's splendid Temple Newsam house and parklands. The tours proved remarkably popular, often requiring ten or more double-deckers. This picture shows Leeds AEC Regent 950 on one of the Leeds tours in March 1967. *Geoffrey Morant*

Sixty more Roe-bodied AEC Regent Vs were taken into stock – ten in 1962 (924-933), fifteen in each of 1963 (934-948) and 1964 (949-963) and a further twenty in 1965 (964-983), which entered service in December 1965 and January 1966, 964-973 therefore having C-suffix registration numbers and 974-983 D suffix ones – they were Leeds' final forward-engined double-deckers. At the Whitkirk terminus of route 39 at Ring Road, Halton, 976 is passed by 946 in this May 1970 view. The orange glow in the upper deck of both vehicles came from the two window panels in the roof which were glazed in orange-tinted glass – the panels had been a feature of Leeds double-deckers since 1962. *Linden Edwards*

Photographed in August 1967 in the revised livery for one-man operation, 45 was the second of four AEC Reliances with Roe dual-entrance bodies new in August 1964. They had a very short life in Leeds, being withdrawn in December 1970. Five similar Reliances (39-43) were delivered in 1962. It is seen operating the hourly service from Temple Newsam to the bus station – this had been one of the last tram routes to close on 7th November 1959. *Geoffrey Morant*

The first rear engined buses to enter the Leeds fleet were ten Daimler Fleetlines with Roe bodies which were delivered in December 1964. The first of the batch, 101, which had been exhibited at the 1964 Commercial Motor Show in October, is pictured on cross-city service 15 from Whingate in the west to Seacroft in the east. It has been converted to one-man operation and repainted in the double-deck version of the reversed livery for one man operated buses. *Roy Marshall*

Wisely, Leeds waited a few years before buying Atlanteans. Ten Weymann-bodied ones, numbered 331-340, entered service in 1965. Bound for Swinnow on the cross-city service from Gipton and in the reversed one man livery, 337, is seen in New Market Street, following 337 is one of the Metro-Cammell bodied AEC Regent Vs new in 1960. *Linden Edwards*

Operating the service from Gipton to Greenthorpe, fleet number 127, a Daimler Fleetline with a Roe body, is seen in the version of the green livery used for crew-operated buses in this April 1967 view. This was one of fifteen in the second batch of Fleetlines which were delivered in 1966. They were converted for one-man operation in early 1973 when they were repainted into the reversed livery. *Geoffrey Morant*

Thirty Leyland Atlanteans (356 – 385) with Park Royal bodies were delivered in September 1968. This is newly delivered 382 in the standard (two man operated) livery at Leeds' new Middleton Garage. This was a copy of Sheffield's East Bank garage and Sheffield had generously allowed Leeds to use its drawings and specifications saving time and fees. It housed 125 buses under cover and opened on 13th November 1966, replacing Hunslet garage which had originally been a tram depot with stables for the horses. *Alan Mortimer*

Leeds standardised on this dual door style of Roe body for its future Atlanteans (386-595) and Fleetlines (146-230) delivered over the years 1968-1974, the last 30 Fleetlines having Leyland engines. This is Roe-bodied Leyland Atlantean 415, from the batch 406-425 new in 1970, photographed at Moortown on the service to Middleton which had replaced the tram service in March 1959. The department was early in using radio communication to control operations – the aerial is attached to the centre pillar of the upper deck front windows and, in this case, hangs down in front of the destination indicator. The radio control system was introduced in 1964, following a 1961 visit to the United States by Deputy Chief Traffic Officer Arnold Stone, who been impressed by its success in Buffalo, New York State. *Alan Mortimer*

In line with the industry trend of 'large one-man operated single-deckers', forty AEC Swifts entered service in 1968. As usual for Leeds, the bodies were sourced from Roe and MCW – 76 – 85 had Roe bodies and 61 – 75 and 86 – 100 had MCW. This 1969 picture of 95 in St Peter's Street on the 61 East End Park circular service shows the forward sloping window pillars – another passing fashion of the time. *Arnold Richardson*

Single-deck 36-foot long Daimler Fleetlines with Park Royal dual entrance bodies were chosen for the 1970 single-deck intake. This July 1970 picture shows 1208 from the batch of 30 (1201-1230,) in the standard livery in Eastgate whilst operating on the 61 East End Park circular service. Numbers 1001-1050 were AEC Swifts with similar bodies. *Roy Marshall*

Twenty AEC Swifts with Roe bodies numbered 1051-1070 were Leeds' only single-deck buses delivered in 1971. In this 1972 picture, 1056 is entering the Central Bus Station on the 224 'Fastaway' service from Swarcliffe. This service, and the 225, was introduced in July 1967 and by running direct and non-stop over a portion of the normal 24 and 25 services the journey time was reduced from 24 minutes to 18 minutes, in an effort to encourage more people to use the bus service rather than cause congestion by using their cars. *Geoffrey Morant*

In November 1970 and in association with the Ministry of Transport, Leeds introduced an experimental service linking the Central Bus Station with the Railway Station in City Square and the West Yorkshire Bus Station in Vicar Lane. Numbered 401 this ran a clockwise circuit through the main shopping areas, by then restricted to pedestrians and authorised vehicles, with thirteen stopping places. The six minibuses, 30 to 35, bought for the service were Mercedes-Benz L406Ds with Williams 'Deansgate' bodies. They seated 13 on perimeter seating with provision for 9 standing passengers. Loading and unloading was speeded up by the fitting of particularly wide entrance doors. There was a flat fare, initially of 3d – 2p from 1971 when the currency was changed to decimal – and the service ran every six minutes between 10.00 am and 4.00 pm on Monday to Saturday with speed in the pedestrian precinct limited to a maximum of 7 m.p.h.

Although much trumpeted, it was not a success. In February 1971 it was stated that £426 only had been taken in fares and each of the five buses was carrying an average of 5.98 passengers per journey – 27.2% of its carrying capacity. The cost to the city had been £12,500, half the cost of the scheme, and the Transport Department stated that it would take five years to recover this amount, let alone driver's wages, running costs and depreciation. There were complaints from pedestrians about the buses in the 'traffic free' areas; on decimalisation the fare had been increased by 60% and this had further reduced what small passenger loading there was. Were all this not enough – many people said it was quicker to walk.

Nevertheless the department persisted and in doing so produced the longest lasting result of the experiment – the livery. Initially this was Leeds' usual Leeds Brunswick Green with ivory as carried by 34 in the left hand picture, but in early 1973 five of the buses were repainted into a revised color scheme shown in the second picture.

The official names for these new colours were Buttermilk and Emerald Green and they were adopted for the West Yorkshire PTE fleet after April 1974 – although the unchanged shade of green was renamed as Verona. *June 1971 Geoffrey Morant; August 1973 Peter Henson/ Omnibus Society*

And here is that verona green livery. Just before it was merged into the West Yorkshire PTE on local government reorganisation on 1st April 1974, Leeds took delivery of a single Leyland National, 1301. This is 1301 in 1976 carrying the Metro brand name adopted by the PTE (at first with local city and town names). *Geoffrey Morant*

Todmorden

Todmorden is situated at the junction of the Burnley, Rochdale and Calder valleys. Early bus routes were operated along the valley bottom roads by Todmorden & District Carriage Company. A Tramways Order was granted but the tramway was never built and in January 1907 the corporation became an early operator of motor buses.

The year 1909 saw the construction of a bus garage at Millwood – it was still in use over one hundred years later. On the 1st January 1931 the Corporation sold a 50% interest in the undertaking to the London Midland & Scottish Railway Company and a Joint Committee was formed. The Brunswick Green livery continued but the town and railway coats of arms were then carried on the vehicles, which were allocated to and owned by either the Railway or the Corporation. Fleet numbers stayed with corporation or railway vehicles – numbers 1-4, 7, 9, 11, 13, 15,18, 20, 23, 25, 26, 29, 30, 33, 34, 36, 37 were only used on corporation-owned buses and 5, 6, 8, 10, 12, 14, 16, 17, 19, 21, 22, 24, 27, 28, 31, 32, 35, 38, 39, 40 on railway-owned. Buses carried the appropriate legal owner – for the railway-owned ones this was the LMS, then British Railways and finally Amalgamated Passenger Transport Ltd, when the railway holding passed to the Transport Holding Company. A new vehicle usually took the number of the bus it replaced and if the outgoing vehicle was not to be disposed of immediately, it would have an X placed in front of its fleet number. From the end of the First World War the fleet was Leyland, most having Leyland bodywork until this became unavailable.

Services were extended to Burnley & Hebden Bridge, Bacup was served from both Todmorden and Burnley, and there was a route from Hebden Bridge to Old Town. A joint service with Keighley Corporation was operated between Hebden Bridge and Keighley. On Saturdays only there was a joint service with Rochdale Corporation between Rochdale and Todmorden.

In 1947 Todmorden had some of Leyland's first PD2s and over the next four years 38 PD2's would be delivered – no new buses were then needed for ten years. From 1961 onwards all purchases were single-deckers, still of Leyland manufacture including five acquired second hand.

From 1946 to 1971 Todmorden's general manager was Ted Metcalfe, who had started with Todmorden as a junior clerk in 1924. With major restructuring of the bus industry in the late 1960s it was agreed that when he retired the Todmorden undertaking would merge with the Halifax Joint Omnibus Committee. Ted Metcalfe retired in the Spring of 1971 and Halifax manager Geoffrey Hilditch became acting manager until the Calderdale Joint Omnibus Committee was formed on 6th September 1971.

This interior view of Todmorden's Millwood depot in 1971 nicely captures the fleet and also the problem of the garage – the cross beams that necessitated lowbridge double-deckers. The depot was constructed in 1908 on land adjacent to the Corporation Gas Department's works and was owned by the latter. It therefore passed to the Gas Board on nationalisation and thereafter was leased from the Gas Board. Left to right are Leyland-bodied PD2s 19, 23, 2, 27, 13, 25, 8 and Willowbrook-bodied Leyland Leopard 10. *David Powell*

Todmorden had the first production PD2/1s to enter service. Eight were delivered in 1947, numbered 9-12, 15/16, 30/31, and this is number 12 in Cattle Market Bus Station in Burnley in 1957. Todmorden operated three services from Burnley – to Littleborough Summit (via Todmorden), to Hebden Bridge (via Todmorden) and to Bacup. The latter service ceased in March 1966 whereupon Ribble commenced a Burnley to Bacup service. The sett-paved Ribble bus station had concrete shelters; there was a gap between the shelters which was the entrance to Ribble's Burnley depot. *Geoffrey Morant*

Fourteen more Leyland PD2/1s with lowbridge Leyland bodywork arrived in 1948, their fleet numbers (1-4, 17, 21, 28-29, 32/33/35-38) filling gaps left by withdrawn vehicles. In this 1969 view smartly turned out number 3 has just left the town centre to travel some four miles along Burnley Road to Portsmouth – then the border between Yorkshire and Lancashire. *Michael Russell*

Deliveries in 1950 were four Leyland-bodied PD2/1s in January and four more in December. Number 6 was one of the January delivery and, along with numbers 5, 8, 14, 19 and 34, was owned by the railways; 18 and 26 were owned by the Corporation. Photographed in July 1969, the bus was leaving for Summit where it would meet a Rochdale Corporation 6 or 6A service, through passengers to Littleborough and Rochdale having to transfer there, except on Saturdays when there was a through service. This vehicle operated for nineteen years in the Todmorden fleet. *Michael Russell*

For years Todmorden's services used on-street bus stops but in the late nineteen fifties after using the Market Ground as a temporary starting point, the town council allowed the parking ground to be converted into what it called a 'Bus Starting Centre'. Seen in April 1971 in what was by then known as the Bus Station, number 24 was one of eight Leyland-bodied PD2/12s delivered in 1951 finished in this modified livery, which they retained on repaint. The fleet renewed, no more buses were bought until 1961. In order to supplement income from fares commercial advertising was introduced in 1960. Two PD2/1s and five PD2/12s including number 24 passed to the Calderdale JOC fleet in 1971, 24 becoming Calderdale 355. It later became a training vehicle and passed as such to the West Yorkshire PTE in April 1974. *John Kaye*

The pictures on this page show the rural nature of those Todmorden routes that did not follow the valley bottom. Here on a damp and misty day in October 1969, number 2 is seen approaching the village of Mankinholes, high up on the hillside between the Walsden and Calder Valleys. *Nicholas Harris*

Copy Pit is the location of this July 1969 view of a well laden number 18 being overtaken by a Hillman Imp on its way to Burnley. The bus would have come through Todmorden from either Hebden Bridge or from Summit. The railway on the right is the line from Yorkshire to Burnley and onward into East Lancashire. *Michael Russell*

Making the acute turn at Pecket Well on the return trip from Old Town to Hebden Bridge is one of Todmorden's Leyland Leopards with East Lancashire bodywork. In 1961 the first of these inaugurated one man operation on this route. In the back ground is Cock Hill moor with a dusting of snow. *David Powell*

After the delivery of the last of the fleet of 38 PD2s, no new vehicles were needed for ten years. In 1961 came the first new single-decker since the Leyland TS8s of 1939 (the last of which had been replaced in 1951). Owned by the railways number 12 entered service in April 1961 and was an East Lancs-bodied Leyland Leopard equipped for one-man operation. June 1966. *Geoffrey Morant*

Two more East Lancs-bodied Leopards arrived in 1962 and two in 1964; there was then a break in deliveries until 1967 when four Leopards were delivered, this time with Willowbrook bodies. Two were bus seated (4, 9) the other two (1, 10) had dual-purpose seating and introduced a new mostly cream livery as seen here in April 1971 on number 1. *John Kaye*

In 1969 Todmorden received what were to be its final new vehicles – six Leyland Leopards with Oldham-built Pennine (Seddon) bodywork. Numbered 6, 8, 14, 19, 22-23, numbers 6 and 8 had dual-purpose seats and were in the cream livery; the other four were bus-seated and finished in green and cream as shown here on number 23, standing at Hebden Bridge Railway Station on the route to Old Town. Todmorden also operated a service from Hebden Bridge to Keighley jointly with the West Yorkshire Road Car Co. *John Kaye*

The 1968 Transport Act resulted in the British Rail interest being transferred to Amalgamated Passenger Transport Ltd – a subsidiary of the government-owned National Bus Company. This involvement was to see the arrival in July 1969 of two Leyland Tiger Cubs from East Midland Motor Services. New in 1956 and 1958 respectively and numbered 11 and 15, the move was partly dictated by finance. Todmorden staff considered them underpowered and they were mainly used on routes along the valley. Number 15 is seen on a wet day in August 1969 in Todmorden bus station. *Nicholas Harris*

In an effort to hasten one-man operation, replace the ageing double-deck fleet and control costs, the relationship with APT was used again and in 1970 three Leopards with Eastern Coach Works bodies were acquired from the Sheffield C ('railway') fleet. With the coming formation of the Calderdale Joint Omnibus Committee, they were the last vehicles to join the Todmorden fleet. All the Leopards and the two Tiger Cubs passed to Calderdale along with seven PD2s. In this June 1971 view, number 2 is emitting a certain amount of smoke as it makes its way along New Road, Hebden Bridge just beyond where the Halifax trams terminated. *Geoffrey Morant*

West Riding

The West Riding Automobile Company Ltd of Belle Isle, Wakefield, started life early in the 1900s as two tram systems based on Wakefield and Castleford. It bought its first buses, Bristols, in the 1920s and the final tram system was abandoned in 1932 although, in contrast to the green of the main bus fleet, the red livery of the Wakefield trams was retained for the fleet of buses replacing the trams – something which lasted into the late 1960s. In the 1930s the company standardised on Leylands and had around 150, mainly with Roe bodies.

During the war some 70 Guy Arabs joined the fleet, West Riding managing to have ones bodied by its preferred body supplier, Roe. These rugged buses, many refurbished in the early 1950s, gave up to 20 years service in all parts of their system. Shortly after the war, most of West Riding's elderly 'red' fleet of Leyland Titan central entrance buses were replaced by similar AEC Regents, then followed by a large number of Leyland-bodied Leylands for the green fleet, mostly low height.

In 1950 West Riding bought its major competitor – J Bullock and Sons (1928) Ltd of Featherstone ('B&S Motor Services'). It had a mixed make fleet of around 170 and the acquisition made West Riding the largest independent bus company with a fleet of over 400, increasing its operating territory eastwards to the Selby and Doncaster areas. Equally importantly, West Riding had managed to keep at bay the Tilling and BET groups, whose companies surrounded its operating territory.

The wartime relationship with Guy Motors was renewed in the mid 1950s with 70 Guy Arab lVs and in 1959 West Riding, particularly Chief Engineer Ron Brooke, became closely involved with Guy Motors in the development of Guy's Wulfrunian. In 1961 West Riding's long serving Managing Director, George Henry Margrave retired – he had seen the transition of the company from trams to buses.

Beset by problems in its South African subsidiary, Guy Motors failed in 1961 and was bought by Jaguar, which already owned Daimler with its increasingly successful Fleetline. Wulfrunian deliveries began but the design was never fully developed by Guy or Jaguar and the consequent severe reliability problems put an intolerable financial strain on West Riding and in October 1967 it was sold to the Transport Holding Company ('THC'), soon to become the National Bus Company ('NBC').

The Wulfrunians were soon replaced by Bristol Lodekkas drafted in from sister THC/NBC companies along with new Leyland Atlanteans, Panthers and Daimler Fleetlines but by 1972 the Bristol RE and VRT had become West Riding's standard. In 1970 the NBC fleets in the area were rationalised as the West Riding Group effectively bringing Yorkshire Woollen, County and West Riding under the same control – the title was more of a geographical one than recognition of the company.

From 1956 to 1969 West Riding had a purpose-built bus station in Cross York Street Leeds for its 'red' fleet services. It replaced the former terminus at the Corn Exchange and was used until 1969 after which the services moved into the main bus station. In the mid 1960s picture on the left is Roe-bodied Guy Wulfrunian 976. One of 35 new in 1963, it had a brief life of seven years. By contrast, 'green' Leyland PD2, 693, one of a batch of 20 new in 1950, gave 19 years service. There were 75 PD2s with Leyland bodies, of which 16 were highbridge – there were very few highbridge vehicles in the 'green' fleet. *Linden Edwards*

Most of West Riding's 'green' services into Leeds terminated at the large Central Bus Station. This picture is of Roe-bodied Leyland TS7c 446, new in 1938, arriving in the twilight of its service life of 19 years. Like most of the prewar TS and TD models supplied to West Riding, Leyland 'Gearless' torque converter transmission was originally fitted – as was usually the case it was later replaced with the more usual crash gearbox. In the background the driver of Roe-bodied Guy Arab 783 has just parked his vehicle in the 'lay-over' bay. *John Kaye*

Guy Arab 586 was one of the many 'utility' buses allocated to West Riding during the war and the company was fortunate that it managed to persuade the government that they were bodied by Roe. They all had relatively long lives, being extensively refurbished. By the side of 586, all-Leyland PD2 314 was new in 1947 to the B&S Motor Service which was acquired by West Riding in 1950. *John May*

When the Leeds-Wakefield trams were converted to buses in 1932, the replacing buses were Leyland TD2 with Roe central entrance bodies and for some reason when it came to replace them, the new fleet of Roe-bodied AEC Regents had the same unusual entrance and stairway arrangement. Numbers 56-64, new 1946, had London-type RT3 chassis (they were the first production RT3 chassis numbers 0961001-009) whereas 65-117 (new 1948/49) had the standard Regent III chassis. The 'tram' buses continued to use a terminus at the Corn Exchange, where fleet number 94 was photographed in June 1956 leaving on the 18 service. The 18 turned off the Wakefield main route 10 at Wood Lane along which it ran to terminate at Rothwell. *Geoffrey Morant*

Although AECs featured in the all double-deck 'red' fleet, the six Roe-bodied Regal IIIs of 1948 were a first for the green fleet with two more the following year. Fleet number 652, the last of the eight, is shown here in Castleford bus station on a local service. All the Regals were withdrawn in 1966. *John May*

When West Riding took over B&S Motor Services of Featherstone in 1950, it doubled their fleet size to over 400 vehicles making them the country's largest independent bus company at that time. B&S themselves were one of the largest independent companies of the day with 170 vehicles and depots in Wakefield, Featherstone, Selby and Doncaster.

The 'amalgamation', as it was officially called, went smoothly although the B&S fleet was very mixed with buses from numerous suppliers – all acquired new. Although both companies used a simple numerical sequence for fleet numbers, no renumbering was necessary. The small depot at Doncaster was closed.

B&S's history was not quite so smooth. The three Bullock brothers, Abraham (Abe), Ernest and Jim were the main family members in the business which had developed from the family fish dealers and fruiterers business, the first bus service beginning in 1913 – when West Riding was operating its first tram system. The eldest brother, Ernest, was the Managing Director but friction quickly developed on how the company should be managed.

Jim set up and ran a base in Wakefield, initially for colliery transport. He started to operate independently, purchasing Leyland vehicles, whilst at Featherstone Ernest bought Albions. Abe looked after a garage base in Pontefract, which eventually became South Yorkshire Motor's depot in Cornmarket. Initial meetings with West Riding about amalgamation came to naught at this time.

The brothers did not agree and in 1928 a High Court action started between them which led to Ernest leaving and purchasing the ailing South Yorkshire Motor Company of Thorpe Audlin, Pontefract. Becoming South Yorkshire Motors, it eventually outlived B&S. The B&S Motor Services company was then reconstituted as J Bullock & Sons (1928) Ltd. Services were developed eastwards to Selby and Doncaster and westwards to Wakefield and Leeds and the fleet grew to over 100. It was very mixed – Leylands, Daimlers, AECs, Albions, Bedfords and wartime Guys. The body makers were just as varied, including Leyland, Duple, Willowbrook, Barnaby (of Hull), Roberts, Roe and some built by B&S itself. After the war things remained much the same – Leylands, Daimlers, AECs, Seddons and bodies by Barnaby, Willowbrook, Roe, Strachan, Leyland and Longford, all of which West Riding inherited – the last B&S vehicles were withdrawn in 1967.

Abraham and Jim both joined West Riding – but became rivals in local Rugby League teams, Jim being President of Wakefield Trinity whilst Abraham had the same post at Featherstone Rovers.

The only known colour photograph of a vehicle in B&S's distinctive livery of maroon, red and cream is this one, taken by C Carter in 1952 in Leeds Central Bus Station some two years after the West Riding takeover. Not yet repainted and still carrying the B&S fleet name, 294 was one of six AEC Regent III with Roe lowbridge bodies which entered service in 1947 as part of a major fleet replacement programme. *C Carter*

There are several pictures of former B&S vehicles in West Riding livery and the nine that follow give an idea of the wide variety that West Riding inherited.

Above New in 1938 Leyland TS8 fleet number 222 started life with a Barnaby 35 seat coach body which Barnaby rebuilt in 1945. In 1956 West Riding fitted it with this Willowbrook body removed from 1947 former B&S Leyland PS1 301 when it was rebodied as a double-decker in 1956. The bus was withdrawn in 1962 – this August 1960 picture shows it in Leeds Central Bus Station. *John Kaye*

Below B&S managed to acquire six Leyland-bodied TD7s, 241-246, in 1940 before things were interrupted by hostilities. Also photographed in Leeds, 241 gave 21 years service and outlasting many of West Riding's own contemporary Leyland TD models. *John Kaye*

Barnaby of Hull, and Willowbrook had long been suppliers of bodywork to B&S. They shared the bodywork on 18 Leyland PS1 single deckers (283-290, 297-306) delivered in 1947/48. Fleet number 288 was one of the 8 Barnaby-bodied ones (283-290) and, later, one of twelve PS1 chassis rebodied as double deckers by Roe in 1956, in which form it gave some ten years further service with West Riding. *Peter Roberts*

Number 298 was one of the ten with Willowbrook bodies. Regularly used on the B&S Wakefield to Blackpool express service, with West Riding they had more mundane duties – mostly on services in the Wakefield area. In this picture it is outside West Riding's garage in Savile Street – its home base which came with the B&S business. *Vic Nutton/Travelens*

New in 1949, 329 was one of two Guy Arab saloons bodied by Roe. They were the last Roe-built bodies for B&S – interestingly lacking the usual Roe 'waistrail' beneath the windows. They were B&S's only post war Guys, their Meadows engines made them the more unusual. *Alan Mortimer*

Two Willowbrook-bodied CVD6 delivered in 1950 (341/42) were the last vehicles purchased by B&S and had the highest fleet numbers. Fitted out as dual purpose vehicles, in addition to service work, 341 was more often used as a coach, including operating the Blackpool service and West Riding's weekend excursion programmes. It is seen here in West Riding's reverse livery, into which it was repainted when West Riding was about to purchase its first coaches in 1952; it ran until 1967. *Travelens/Vic Nutton*

Daimler was one of the major chassis suppliers to B&S in postwar years supplying 26 CVD6 chassis. Roe-bodied 325 was one of six obtained in 1949. Three of them enabled the satellite depots at Selby and Doncaster to replace elderly Titans and Regents used on the longer routes – York to Doncaster and Leeds to Goole and 325 was based at Selby until replaced by West Riding highbridge PD2s shortly after the takeover. It was then allocated to Featherstone depot, it is shown here in Doncaster on a service to Pontefract. *John Kaye*

As mentioned in a previous caption, twelve former B&S 1947 PS1 chassis were rebodied by Roe in 1956 to alleviate a shortage of double deckers. Although somewhat underpowered, they were ideal for the flat terrain around Selby where most of them operated and gave West Riding an extra ten years service. This is 798, formerly Willowbrook-bodied 306. *John May*

In 1949 B&S started an association with Seddon, ordering four lightweight buses to replace utility Bedford OWBs used for rural services particularly around Selby where Cawood river bridge was weight restricted. Two (334/35) were delivered in 1950 before the takeover and West Riding took delivery of the other two, which were numbered 707/08 in the West Riding series. Some joint development with Seddon on a 32-seater lightweight then followed, starting in 1952. The prototype was numbered 738 in the West Riding fleet. After two years it went back to Seddon and was replaced by this full-size Perkins R6-engined Seddon Mark 11; numbered 751 it had a Nudd Bros & Lockyer (Duple Midland) body. It ran for nine years and is seen here in 1962 at Selby depot. The development work with a manufacturer was, maybe, a foretaste of things to come. *Peter Roberts*

The 'green' fleet received the first and only AEC Regents in 1952 when ten were delivered – this is number 719. They had Siddall-Hilton 'Morseat' staggered seating on the upper deck – one pair of seats of the rows of four being slightly set back from the other with the aim of giving a little more space to the cramped nature of the low bridge side-gangway configuration. All had gone by 1966. *John May*

In 1952 West Riding bought its first 30ft-long single deckers. Although underfloor engined-chassis were very much the usual thing by then, there were good reasons for the choice of the forward-engined Leyland PS2. Underfloor-engined buses of the time were of greater overall height and West Riding operated many colliery services where overhead pipelines were a hazard. All 28 had Roe bodies, six of them coaches. This is, 737, the last of the service buses in Leeds Central Bus Station in August 1968. *John Kaye*

Ten Roe-bodied PD2/22s entered service in 1954, their bodies were lowbridge. Bound for Leeds on the 'not tram' service, this is number 756 in Wakefield bus station in August 1963 with similarly-bodied Guy Arab behind it. The red-painted wheels were a notable feature of the West Riding fleet – they were continued until the National Bus Company poppy red livery (with grey wheels) replaced the green and cream. *John Kaye*

There was a marked change of vehicle policy in 1955 when West Riding changed allegiance from Leyland to Guy for double-deckers and AEC for single-deckers. Numbers 762-786 were 25 Guy Arabs with Gardner 6LW engines and Roe lowbridge bodies – this picture shows 764 in Castleford depot yard in July 1969. *John Kaye*

West Riding was late in finally going down the 'underfloor' route after a single AEC Regal IV (709) in 1950. Nineteen AEC Reliances were delivered in 1956/57, 799-805 having Roe's 'Dalesman' coach body whilst 806-817 had Roe bus bodies – with 44 seats these had just 9 seats less than the lowbridge double-deck Arabs. Top is fleet number 813 and centre is 802. *October 1969 Geoffrey Morant; c1966 Nicholas Harris*

In 1961 the first one man operated (OMO) vehicles were introduced at Selby and Belle Isle (Wakefield) depots. Twelve dual-door Roe-bodied AEC Reliances (920-931) were bought for this purpose. Here, 921 is entering Wakefield Bus Station in 1967. Fleet numbers 863-913 were the first of the Guy Wulfrunians which had such an important role in the company's history. Their pictures follow. *Peter Henson/Omnibus Society*

West Riding's deep but maybe unfortunate involvement in the development of the Wulfrunian is well documented, as are the misfortunes of Guy Motors which led to its insolvency and 1961 acquisition, for very little money, by Jaguar which also owned Daimler. Had Guy not got into financial difficulties it seems unlikely that the Wulfrunian would have fared much better for it was a case of the simultaneous introduction of too many pieces of new technology.

Delivered in 1959 in 'tramway red', the prototype Guy Wulfrunian 863 spent a short time on demonstration work for Guy Motors before arriving at West Riding. Pictures just after arrival at Belle Isle, where it was based, the firm posed it next to the fleet's then oldest Guy – a utility Arab which had been rebodied with a 1939 Roe body from a Leyland TD5. Two other utility Guy Arabs had received similar treatment. .

These front and rear views of 863 were taken in September 1968 by which time it had lost the rather attractive original front grille and been repainted green. Following the well publicised technical problems with the Wulfrunian, particularly with the front suspension, in 1968 863 (and others) had their seating capacity reduced from 75 to 67. By the early 1970s, the requirement for a 'red' fleet had gone and all the fleet was painted in green livery. *Peter Roberts (upper); John Kaye (lower)*

In all 150 Wulfrunians were ordered – 23 in 1959, 27 in 1960, 20 in 1961, 25 in 1962, 30 in 1963 and 25 in 1964. They were numbered 864-913, 939-955, 960-984 and 1000-1029 – prototype 863 appears to have been outside the main orders . West Riding also bought two for County, which it owned jointly with the BET group.

Above By the time 957 arrived for the 'red' fleet in 1963 nearly one hundred had been delivered, the extent of the technical problems had become very clear. Behind it, in Wakefield Bus Station in September 1968, 'green' model 939 has been repainted in the darker Tilling green, the final colour configuration for the Wulfrunians introduced in 1968 when the firm was bought by the Transport Holding Company. An odd feature of the West Riding Wulfrunians were the front indicator winding handles, which were on the outside of the body at the top of the nearside windscreen; a grab handle and step (visible in this picture) were provided for the conductor to reach them. *John Kaye*

Below Fleet number 1003, delivered in 1965 and seen here entering Pontefract Bus Station in July of that year, was among the last Wulfrunians to be delivered. By this time West Riding had cancelled the final order for 25 and replaced it with one for Leyland Atlanteans with Roe bodies. *Alan Mortimer*

The Wulfrunian found little success elsewhere and several quickly passed to West Riding. In all, West Riding eventually owned 132 of the production run of 137, although two were early demonstrators and only acquired for spares.

After two years service with West Wales Motors of Ty Croes, Carmarthen, XBX 350, was acquired by West Riding in 1963. Numbered 959 it is pictured in Wakefield Bus Station in a reversed variation of the standard livery. It was one of five production Wulfrunians to receive East Lancs bodies and gave a further six years service life before going for scrap. *John May*

Lancashire United Transport ordered three and, having got the first, promptly cancelled the other two. After two years (in which it saw little use), LUT sold it to West Riding (number 938). West Riding had a casual relationship with LUT, also independent and of similar size, the two sharing some directorships in their early days. Withdrawn in 1968, 938 was the only Wulfrunian bodied by Northern Counties and here is seen leaving Leeds for the circuitous route to Woolley Moor. *Photobus*

There were, however, some conventional vehicles. From 1964 West Riding built up a sizeable fleet of standard 'off the peg' Bedford coaches, most with Plaxton bodies. In 1966 a separate number series was begun for them, starting at 1. This is number 10, a Bedford VAM in the queue of coaches leaving Doncaster Races in September 1971. *Roy Marshall*

With their ever increasing problems, the final order for Wulfrunians was cancelled and replaced with one for 25 Leyland Atlantean PDR1/2 with Roe bodies which were delivered in March to June 1966. This is the first of them, when new, in Leeds bus station on the trunk 67 service to Sheffield. *Geoffrey Morant*

West Riding bought another dose of problems when it ordered the first production models of the Cummins-engined Daimler 'Roadliner'. Numbered 126-135, their Plaxton bodies were good enough but the then unfamiliar Cummins engine did not run well in the Roadliner and they were all withdrawn after short service life of seven years. There were no more Roadliners but there was more trouble ahead with the next two batches of single-deckers which were Leyland Panthers and AEC Swifts. *Alan Mortimer*

None of the early rear-engined single-decker models was over reliable and, with the problems of the Wulfrunians, caution might have been expected. Far from it. Comments from West Riding staff suggested that the single deck buses acquired in this period were some of the most unreliable since the early 1930s.

The unproven Roadliners were followed in 1967 by ten Leyland Panthers (136-145), then six AEC Swifts (19-24), 10 more Panthers (146-155) and then a further 25 (156-180). The body order was similarly mixed – Roe for 136-145 and 156-165 and Marshall for the rest.

Top to bottom Marshall-bodied AEC Swift 23 in Dewsbury bus station, March 1969. Roy Marshall

Panther 150, also Marshall bodied, departing the Piccadilly terminus in York in June 1968 – the route to Selby and Doncaster was one inherited from B&S in 1950. *Geoffrey Morant*

The Roe-bodied Panthers looked very different. Taken at Pontefract Bus Station, having made the long journey from Holmfirth, 165 is parked alongside 1957 Guy Arab 827. *Peter Henson/Omnibus Society*

By now in financial difficulties, on 30th October 1967 the company was sold to the Transport Holding Company, which owned most of the country's buses. The fleet was a problem but the operating territory and services were valuable.

The 1969 deliveries, ordered before the company was sold, more or less completed the catalogue of manufacturer's offerings. Numbers 32-34 (1968) were Plaxton-bodied Leyland Leopards fitted out with coach seats. *May 1969 Roy Marshall*

There were five Plaxton-bodied Leyland Panthers (236-240, renumbered 277-281 in 1971), which looked much the same as Roe-bodied 156-165, and they were followed by 241-245 (renumbered 282-286 in 1971) – Plaxton-bodied Bristol RELL6G. *March 1972 Roy Marshall*

Variety continued in double-deckers with a change from Atlanteans to Fleetlines. Fleet numbers 181-210 (1968) and 211-235 (1969) were Roe-bodied Daimler Fleetlines with Gardner 6LX engines. *October 1969, Geoffrey Morant*

The first priority for the THC and its successor, the National Bus Company ('NBC') was to bring in vehicles from elsewhere and eliminate the Wulfrunians. The first went in 1968 and by 1972 they were all gone.

The first buses to be drafted in were four 18-month old Northern Counties-bodied Fleetlines from the Mexborough & Swinton fleet (246-249). Commencing in 1969 a large fleet of elderly Bristol Lodekkas were drafted in from sister NBC companies – 42 LD6G from Midland General/Mansfield & District, 8 LD6G from Lincolnshire and 28 FLF6G from Bristol Omnibus; Halifax's five Dennis Lolines were purchased.

Top to bottom In Wakefield bus station in May 1969 were former Mexborough and Swinton Fleetline 247, alongside Wulfrunian 895 and former Midland General Lodekka 402 and, on the far left, Atlantean 122.

428 was from the Lincolnshire Road Car Company and is seen on a Wakefield, Castleford to Pontefract service, having just left Wakefield bus station. *Geoffrey Morant*

456 was one of the FLFs from Bristol Omnibus, seen here in Dewsbury in May 1970. *Peter Henson/ Omnibus Society*

Below in May 1972 is former Halifax Loline 552. Originally 467 it was renumbered 552 in the 1970 fleet renumbering when the Yorkshire Woollen, West Riding and Hebble's coach fleet were combined under one management. *John Kaye*

In 1971 twelve Alexander bodied Daimler Fleetlines joined the fleet. Numbered 273-284 (later 671-682) they were similar to those being delivered to other THC fleets and were followed by 25 with Northern Counties bodies in 1972. This picture shows brand new 281 in Leeds.
Geoffrey Morant

From 1969 to 1972 44 standard ECW-bodied Gardner-engined Bristol RELLs joined the fleet. This is 294 (originally 257) of the 1970 batch, pictured in Pontefract, followed by Ford of Ackworth's Willowbrook-bodied Leyland Leopard CYG 423H.
Peter Henson/Omnibus Society

The days of variety and experiment were over. Future deliveries would be standard National Bus Company Bristol VRs and Leyland Nationals. This is 735, the first of the 1973 delivery of 12, pictured in Selby on its first day in service .

Given the choice of NBC leaf green or poppy red the combined West Riding and Yorkshire Woollen companies selected red.

It was somehow fitting that West Riding once again had a 'red' fleet.
Peter Henson/Omnibus Society

123

West Yorkshire Road Car Co

Based in the elegant spa town of Harrogate, the West Yorkshire Road Car Company's operating territory was a mixture of urban and rural, the latter serving much of the Yorkshire Dales. It originated in 1906 as the Harrogate Road Car Company Ltd, the Tilling and BAT groups acquired major shareholdings as did the LMS and LNER railways in 1929. Numerous acquisitions ahead of the 1930 Road Traffic Act gave it footholds throughout Airedale and also in York and Grassingtom, with principal depots in Keighley, Bradford, Leeds, Harrogate and York.

There were two important subsidiary fleets, which carried appropriate fleetnames and prefixes to their fleet numbers. Keighley-West Yorkshire Services Limited was registered jointly with Keighley Corporation in 1932 and lasted until 1975. In 1934 York-West Yorkshire Joint Services was formed to take over the constrained municipal services in that city – it was wound up in 1986.

The fleet was typically Tilling. Tilling Stevens saloons formed the early fleet, the 1927-1930 acquisitions added an array of chassis makes, then came a Dennis Lancet and Leyland Titan interlude after which its fleet in the post-war years was around 270 double-deck and 200 single-deck and 50 or so coaches – firmly Bristol chassis with Eastern Coachworks bodies, finished in Tilling red. A particular feature was the 'bible-type' indicator displays – hinged metal sheets with the details painted on – which lasted until 1958.

For many years it was managed by Major F J Chapple. He moved to take charge at Bristol in 1950 and it was probably no surprise when West Yorkshire was allocated the second prototype Bristol Lodekka – it was exhibited at the 1951 Festival of Britain. H N Tuff then became General Manager until 1967 when he was succeeded by the long-serving Traffic Manager, J W Lawrence – their management followed Tilling practice although there were several innovations not least the first Dial a Ride minibus services using Ford Transits.

A major acquisition in 1967 was the business of Samuel Ledgard. After formation of the National Bus Company in 1969, West Yorkshire took over three of Hebble's Bradford area routes in May 1970. The 1974 formation of the West Yorkshire PTE had a major effect upon the company's operations at which point the book's coverage ends. A joint Metro-National Management Company was formed in 1978; from 1981 many WYRCC buses carried its fleetname and by 1984 its Verona Green & Buttermilk livery.

In 1950/51 31 ECW-bodied Bristol LL5G saloons joined the fleet. Of the newly permitted 30ft length they had 39 seats instead of the 35 of earlier L5G saloons. 23 had 7ft 6in-wide bodies, including SGL 9 shown here; the others were 8ft outrigged on a 7ft 6in chassis. SGL9 (numbered 409 when new) was garaged for many years at Skipton or neighbour Grassington. In this picture it is passing the Tennant Arms Hotel at Kilnsey, with the formidable Kilnsey Crag in the background, on the picturesque Wharfedale route 71 from Buckden to Skipton, probably on the 8.15 am journey from Buckden. Later in the 1950s the single adult fare from here to Skipton Railway Station would have been 1s 10d. *Photobus/ Arnold Richardson*

Harrogate-based SG119 (originally 224) was a 35-seater 1947 Bristol L5G, pictured here working a Harrogate local service between Oatlands and New Park. Originally with a timber-framed body, most of the batch was rebuilt with new metal-framed sides after deterioration of the unseasoned timber used in the original frame and, so treated, SG119 lasted until late 1964, perhaps helped by a relatively easy life in Harrogate. The letters in the fleet number indicated vehicle type (S – single-deck, D – double-deck) followed by the engine make (B – Bristol, G – Gardner). *John May*

The Keighley-West Yorkshire fleet had a K-prefix to the fleet number. In this picture Bristol K6B KDB26 is in North Street, Keighley. Most Keighley local services worked cross-town, the 22 running from Bracken Bank Avenue to Stockbridge on the Bradford Road. The Bristol-engined K6B engine was more powerful than the K5G's Gardner 5LW. Better suited to the hilly terrain on the south side of Keighley they also gave a lively performance on the flat. The fleet was always very well turned out and it seems hard to believe that KDB26 was withdrawn and sold for scrap in September 1964, a few weeks after this picture was taken. *John May*

KSGL22 was a 1951 Bristol LL5G (all the fleet had ECW bodies unless otherwise noted) from the same batch as SGL9, shown previously. This bus, however, went new to Keighley-West Yorkshire Services, whose fleet name it carries. It is in Keighley Bus Station at the stand for Silsden. The location was close to the one-time terminus of the trolleybus service which opened in 1924. By 1932, the year the joint company was formed, it was obsolete and was quickly abandoned. Despite the unhelpful indicator setting, KSGL22 is probably working service 12 – an interesting service which ran from Haworth, down the Worth Valley to Keighley and up the Aire Valley to Steeton and Silsden. Hourly, it continued through to Addingham, where it followed the Wharfe Valley down to Ilkley. Whilst providing a useful through service, the route was followed much of the way by more local services. Withdrawn in 1966, the bus passed to a Huddersfield contractor. *John May*

Ribble's fleet of 'White Lady' double-deck coaches had proved successful and West Yorkshire decided to try something similar. In April 1952 3-year old Bristol K6B 751 was so converted, painted cream with red relief. For the 1953 season it was joined by Bristol KSW6B 851, LWR 417, painted black & silver with abundant polished metal trim. At the end of the 1953 season, 751 was altered back to a normal bus but for the 1954 season, 851 was repainted in the red and cream shown in this picture, taken in the mid to late 1950s. Visible are its Perspex panels in the roof and the absence of opening side windows because it was fitted with what was described as 'air-conditioning'; the raised line of the rear lower deck window was to allow a rack for luggage. 851 became DBW31 on renumbering in April 1954. By around 1960 it had been demoted to bus use, working from York, with plain livery to suit and looking rather incongruous having retained its decorative trim. Perhaps not surprisingly, it became the first of the KSWs to be withdrawn – in 1964. It went onto to a somewhat appropriate second life with Regent Bingo in Batley. *Photobus/Arnold Richardson*

New in 1952, KSW6B DBW20 (new as 838) had a more normal life. Seen here working from Bradford depot, it is exiting the modern Market Place at Shipley, through which all Bradford inbound/outbound services were diverted on its opening in June 1957. After crossing this bridge over the railway from Shipley up the Aire Valley to Skipton, DBW20 will run down to cross the River Aire at Baildon Bridge and then climb the taxing Hollins Hill on its way to Guiseley and Ilkley – the bus had been fitted with rear platform doors in 1954/55 for these longer runs. In 1957 the 63 service ran half-hourly but would to suffer severe competition from the regular DMU train service. The revised indicator layout eliminated the 'via' display was fitted in 1963. The bus was withdrawn in December 1967, a few months after this photograph. *Nicholas Harris*

Pictured here passing Bootham Bar in York in June 1968, York-West Yorkshire highbridge Bristol K5G, YDG87, was not quite what it seems. It and ten others were extensive rebuilds in 1955 of K5Gs new in 1939. The running units of the earlier chassis were reconditioned, the chassis frame had new sides, justifying a new chassis and registration number. Fitted with a new ECW body it re-entered service in May 1956. Service 2 ran every 15 minutes from Bur Dyke Avenue to Cornlands Road. Behind is 1966 Bristol Lodekka FS6B YDX219 on service 9 to Tang Hall Lane. *Geoffrey Morant*

New in 1956, EUG52 was a Bristol LS5G. Its ECW body had 41 express-type seats and reversed livery. Like many express coaches within a bus body shell, it was demoted to stage carriage duties by 1959. The photograph shows it in its post-1965 role – repainted in bus livery and with the 45 bus seats fitted in that year. Renumbered SMG52 it spent its later days on Harrogate locals, as here in Harrogate Bus Station on route 8 to Claro Road. Although not confirmed officially, the 'M' in the fleet number is believed to have signified 'maximum' seating. *John May*

New in 1959 DX81, seen here in early August 1960, was one of the last batch of the LD model. Leeds based and working the 36 service from Harrogate, it is pictured on Vicar Lane in the city approaching the Vicar Lane Bus Station used by West Yorkshire. A characteristic of the Lodekka in the 1950s, when the conventional 'K' type was mixed in with them on service, was the habit of passengers, and conductors, to lurch forward on entering the lower saloon, forgetting there was no step into the lower saloon. They were popular, too, in cold weather – on the 67 service between Crossflatts and Bradford they proved warm and fast during the early 1963 freezing weather, when passengers often paid the higher fare in preference to a ride on Bradford's unheated trolleybuses. *John Kaye*

New in 1962, KDX140 was an FS6B – the K-prefix indicated it was the property of Keighley-West Yorkshire Services. Seen here in Bronte country at the Haworth terminus of service 12 to Keighley, it was one of a batch of 26 delivered in 1962/63 numbered KDX136-145, YDX146-149 (for York) and DX150-161 for the main fleet. Unlike many operators, West Yorkshire was never bothered about booking registration numbers which coincided with fleet numbers. *Photobus/Arnold Richardson*

In 1950/51 31 ECW-bodied Bristol LL5G saloons joined the fleet. Of the newly permitted 30ft length they had 39 seats instead of the 35 of earlier L5G saloons. 23 had 7ft 6in-wide bodies, including SGL 9 shown here; the others were 8ft outrigged on a 7ft 6in chassis. SGL9 (numbered 409 when new) was garaged for many years at Skipton or neighbour Grassington. In this picture it is passing the Tennant Arms Hotel at Kilnsey, with the formidable Kilnsey Crag in the background, on the picturesque Wharfedale route 71 from Buckden to Skipton, probably on the 8.15 am journey from Buckden. Later in the 1950s the single adult fare from here to Skipton Railway Station would have been 1s 10d. *Photobus/Arnold Richardson*

The Keighley to Riddlesden local service required a light vehicle – the route crossed a wooden bridge over the Leeds & Liverpool Canal and then (until 1954) followed a narrow road with a 'V' bend. Subsequently the route was varied but one-man operation was a necessity. For such duties West Yorkshire had a fleet of Albion-engined Bristol SUL4A with 36-seat ECW bodies (SMA1-18, new 1962-1965). Seen here in Keighley in July 1967, this is SMA16; the FS6B (KDX142) is about to pull out for the climb up the Worth Valley to Oxenhope. *Travelens/Vic Nutton*

Bristol REs were introduced into the fleet in 1964. Those with bus bodies were numbered from SRG1 and had reached SRG152 by the time the fleet was renumbered into 'thousands' blocks in October 1971 and most were single door. SRG23 of 1966 and SRG 34-38 of 1967 were dual door. Seen here in August 1967, its the 'Pay As You Enter' sign clearly visible, SRG34 was working the then hourly Harrogate local service 7A arriving from Cornwall Road and turning into Station Parade, Harrogate, before continuing to Pannal Railway Station. The 7A would soon be altered with buses from Cornwall Road running to Pannal Ash, whilst Pannal Railway Station duties commenced from the bus station. *Alan Mortimer*

Quite a change from the endless Bristols were the Leyland-engined Bedford VAM14s delivered in 1967 – although they still had ECW bodies. There were four in the batch, SML 1-4, of which this is the first, seen here working a private duty. Something of a stop gap until Bristol's lightweight LH chassis was available, they had a relatively short life, passing into the reserve fleet in 1972, by which time they had been renumbered 1147-1150. *Nicholas Harris*

With the Lodekka no longer available and one-man operation becoming increasingly important, the company's first Bristol VRs (and its first 30ft-long double deckers) entered service in 1969. One of the first batch, VR10 (later 1910) is at Saltaire roundabout on the 10-minute frequency route 67 from Bradford to Keighley, one journey hourly continuing to Skipton as in this 1969 view. The roundabout was the terminus of Bradford's trolleybus service 40 – one can just be seen in Saltaire Road on the left of the picture. *Nicholas Harris*

At the end of October 1972, WYRCC was the first in this country to introduce a 'Dial and Ride' (as the system was known in the United States) service. Named 'Chauffeur Coach' the idea was to encourage shoppers to leave their cars at home by the provision of comfortable small and flexible vehicles. There were five basic routes in the Harrogate and Knaresborough area and passengers could telephone the control centre before their journey so that the centre could instruct the driver to divert from his primary route to pick them up. Two 15-seat Williams Deansgate-bodied Ford Transits were hired, equipped with two-way radios and numbered 1115/16. Seen in Harrogate in June 1973 this is the second of the pair. The trial was a success, leading to the purchase of the pair after twelve months. It was a truly pioneering innovation – quite startling for its time and stimulated the wider use of minibuses and the 'ring and ride' concept of later years. *Geoffrey Morant*

Opposite top From 1969 the Bristol LH was the group's vehicle for lighter duties and West Yorkshire took delivery of 26 in 1969. They had Leyland engines and seated 45. In this June 1970 picture LH8 was 'parked off' at Harrogate Bus Station, having come in from Knaresborough on the 17 service. The green dot by its fleet number shows its home depot was Harrogate – the other colours used were grey – Keighley, blue – Bradford –, maroon – Leeds and yellow – York.

Opposite West Yorkshire had relatively few joint services and this one, service 9 from Colne to Keighley, jointly worked with Burnley, Colne and Nelson Joint Transport Committee ('BCN'), had an interesting history. It had been started by early pioneer operator, Ezra Laycock & Sons, of Barnoldswick (who appear elsewhere in this book). In April 1934 Laycock sold the service to BCN and Keighley-West Yorkshire purchased a share to maintain its interests in the area. This picture, taken in November 1969, at Heifer Lane terminus in Colne, shows both operators' vehicles on the service. Bristol RELL6G, KSRG95, new that month, is pulling onto the stand whilst the driver of BCN's East Lancs-bodied Leyland Tiger Cub 58, new in 1963, reads his newspaper during layover time. The code 'KSRG' may seem long but it was meaningful to crews and garage staff – '**K**eighley **S**ingle-decker **R**ear-engined **G**ardner engine' – perhaps more so than the 2295 that it became when the fleet was renumbered in October 1971 – the computer, however, would have found it easier! *Geoffrey Morant*

Yorkshire Woollen

Based in Dewsbury, The Yorkshire (Woollen District) Electric Tramways Ltd ('Yorkshire Woollen' or 'YWD') was registered by the British Electric Traction Company in November 1901 and its first tram service operated in February 1903; by April 1904 there were seventeen miles of track and 58 trams. The only local authority in the immediate area to have an independent (steam) tramway was Batley Corporation which leased it to Yorkshire Woollen in 1905. Motor bus operation started in 1913 to connect the Yorkshire Woollen system at Ravensthorpe with the Huddersfield Corporation's tramway at Bradley and to start a motorbus service from Scholes to Cleckheaton.

The initial fleet was Daimler, Leylands were then chosen until the mid 1920's, 45 Dennis single deckers joining the fleet between 1925 and 1928. In 1926, along with West Riding and Yorkshire Traction, YWD bought an equal share in County Motors of Lepton. In anticipation of tramway abandonment the company bought its first double-deck vehicles in 1928. A bus station was opened in Asman Square, Dewsbury, in 1932 and would serve for many decades.

The tramways closed at the end of October 1934 the company's name being changed to Yorkshire Woollen District Transport Co Ltd ('YWD'), although the fleetname on the sides of buses was simply 'Yorkshire'. By 1935 the fleet had expanded to 224 vehicles. Early in the Second World War YWD was fortunate to be allocated a number of Leyland double-deckers but thereafter its allocation was Guy Arabs – 61 would join the fleet between 1942 and 1947.

During the 1950s there was extensive rebodying of vehicles, including rebodying single-deckers to double-deckers. In 1953 the maroon & cream livery used since tramway days was changed to all-over red, coaches being cream with red relief. The fleet remained Leyland but when the increase in the maximum length of double deckers to 30ft was authorised in 1956 orders were placed for AEC Regent Vs. Rear-engined double-deckers arrived in 1965 in anticipation of one man operation.

Yorkshire Woollen's network was intense and industrial, connecting most of the industrial towns and cities in the West Riding and although not large – its fleet was about 250 – it was very profitable, ridership reaching a peak of 80.2 million in 1964. One manager described it as 'the BET's goldmine'.

Along with the rest of the BET group it became part of the National Bus Company in 1969 and, prompted in part by West Riding's problems, from 1970 there was reorganisation also involving Hebble, County and West Riding to create common management with West Riding Automobile Company. The head office moved to West Riding's premises at Wakefield – but Yorkshire Woollen's staff were firmly in charge.

The war over, Yorkshire Woollen was in need of substantial investment in new buses and in 1948 just under one hundred new Leylands were delivered. The pre-war fleet had been largely single-deck and the new 558-638 were single-deckers. The other fifteen (543-557) were PD2s with Brush bodywork. In this rare colour view taken in 1950, 545 is pictured on Sovereign Street, Leeds. The building in the background is Leeds City Transport's Swinegate depot. The dark maroon livery began to be phased out from 1953, to be replaced by an overall red livery. The driver is completing his paperwork before the return journey to Dewsbury. *C. Carter*

The single-deck deliveries in 1948 were Leyland PS1s with bodywork by Brush to the then current BET Federation standard design. In 1960 numbers 621/22 were converted for towing and, numbered E5 & E6, they performed this duty until November 1969. This is E5 seen outside the Saville Town, Dewsbury garage and works a few months before it was sold. *Omnibus Society/Peter Henson*

With larger single-deckers available in the 1950s, the 34-seat Leyland PS1s were less useful and in 1954/55 twenty four were rebodied with new Metro Cammell double-deck bodies. Fleet number 574 was one of the 1955 batch and would see a further twelve years of service. Chester Street Bus Station in Bradford is the location of this 1959 view – bus was working the long service from Bradford to Sheffield, jointly operated with Yorkshire Traction and Sheffield. Drawn up behind is similar rebody – a Yorkshire Traction Northern Counties-rebodied PS2. In the background North Western Weymann-bodied Bristol L5G 298 was bound for Oldham on a duplicate short working on the joint Yorkshire Woollen / North Western X12 service to Manchester. *Geoffrey Morant*

The first underfloor-engined single-deckers for Yorkshire Woollen were five Leyland Royal Tigers with Brush bodywork. The first was one the first production Royal Tigers; numbered 734 it was displayed at the 1950 Commercial Motor Show. The remaining four (693-696) were delivered in 1951. Fleet numbers were in one generally chronological sequence but were allocated on ordering and delivery delays could mean they were out of sequence when they arrived. This 1962 picture shows 695 in a crowded Dewsbury bus station working the D1 service to Ossett.
Peter Roberts

Alongside the Royal Tigers were ten Leyland-MCW Olympics, 688-692 and 735-739. Mechanically similar to the Royal Tigers, the Olympic was integrally-constructed using Leyland mechanical units in a frame by Weymann, which at the time shared a sales organisation with Metro Cammell – 'MCW' in this case meaning Metropolitan Cammell-Weymann. They ran until 1965. *Peter Roberts*

Before the arrival of the Royal Tigers and Olympics, Yorkshire Woollen had taken 37 Leyland PS2s into stock in 1950, together with six OPD2 chassis which were also bodied as single-deckers. Eight (682-687, 726/27) were Windover-bodied coaches and 29 (697-725) plus OPD2s 727-733 had bus bodies by Willowbrook. To increase seating, in 1955 all the bus-bodied ones had their 27ft 6in chassis and body lengthened to 30ft by Willowbrook and seating capacity increased to 38, being repainted into the mostly cream livery illustrated in this August 1963 picture of 721 at Cleckheaton. *Travelens/Vic Nutton*

In 1963 six of the 1950 Leyland Tiger PS2s (697-700/8/9) had their lengthened Willowbrook bodies removed, their chassis were shortened to 27ft and then sent to Roe for new double-deck bodies. The whole fleet was renumbered in 1967, the double-deck rebodied PS1s becoming 36-47 and the PS2s 48-53. This is 53 (formerly 709) outside Saville Town garage in August 1968. Its indicator display is set for a local service but at busy times it was not unusual to see these vehicles working the X12 service across the Pennines from Bradford to Manchester. *Alan Mortimer*

During the Second World War new buses were allocated by the Ministry of Supply. Yorkshire Woollen's allocation was 27 Guy Arabs (all but one with 8.4-litre 6LW Gardner engines) and 8 Daimler CWA6 all with 'utility' bodies. Twenty three of the Guys were rebodied by Roe over the years 1952-1955. This picture is of 503 in Calder Road, Dewsbury, in 1966. New in 1944 its original body was Weymann. *Nicholas Harris*

The eight Daimlers never arrived. Not wanting to add another make to the fleet and maybe concerned about their performance in YWD's hilly terrain, an exchange was arranged with fellow BET group member Maidstone and District which had just put into service eight new 6LW-engined Guy Arabs. The Daimlers went new to Maidstone, where they got Kent registration numbers and the Kent-registered Guys came to Yorkshire. Numbered 506-513 they were rebodied by Roe over the years 1952-1956. In this picture inside Dewsbury garage in 1962 are 508 and 507. YWD's Guys ran until 1965/67. *Peter Roberts*

Bought by YWD in 1956, Leyland PD2 773 (later 54) was new in 1954 and had spent its first two years on demonstration duties for Leyland Motors. Its had a lightweight Metro-Cammell body and was built with and to the same specification as Edinburgh's second batch of 100 such vehicles. In the spring of 1969 when there were weight restrictions on North Bridge in Halifax, it spent two months in the Hebble fleet where it was numbered 254. It was withdrawn in 1970. In this 1968 picture it stands by the main door of Yorkshire Woollen's head office at Saville Town. *Alan Mortimer*

From 1956 to 1962 Yorkshire Woollen changed from buying Leylands to AECs with Reliance single-deckers and Regent V forward-entrance 30ft-long double-deckers. Metro Cammell-bodied Regents 786-795 entered service in 1958 followed by 796-810 in 1959 – their unrelieved red livery did little to enhance the appearance of the fleet. This March 1959 view shows 791 in Mill Street, Dewsbury, outside the depot. *Geoffrey Morant*

AEC Regent Vs continued to be the choice for double-decker purchases and in 1961 a further ten (842-861, later 89-98) were delivered, this time the order for bodywork being placed with Northern Counties. In April 1972 this picture is of number 93 in Dewsbury Bus Station, awaiting departure to Pudsey. *Roy Marshall*

In 1962 orders reverted to Leyland with nine PD3As, two Leopard coaches and fifteen Leopard buses. Numbered 890-898 the PD3As had Metro-Cammell bodywork and became 99-107 in the 1967 renumbering. Here 104 is pictured outside Ings Grove Park in Mirfield taking standing time before working service 20 to Leeds via Heckmondwike. *Linden Edwards*

The 1964 double-decker order was placed with Leyland group company Albion for fourteen low-height Lowlander chassis with Weymann bodies. As was usual for Lowlanders supplied in England, they were badged as Leylands. They were numbered 926-939, becoming 108-121 in 1967). In this March1967 view in Dewsbury Bus Station 114 is working service B. T Rather than being numbered, Yorkshire's former tram services around Dewsbury were lettered A to M, occasionally followed by a number; newer and longer routes were numbered. The bus has an illuminated advertisement panel – a fashion of the time. *Geoffrey Morant*

Leyland Leopards continued to be the choice for single-deckers. Seen leaving Cullingworth on the long route 2 from Keighley to Ossett via Halifax and Dewsbury, 957 was one of 28 Weymann-bodied Leopards new in 1964. The mostly cream livery was used on single-deckers delivered between 1959 and 1966. *Nicholas Harris*

YWD's first rear-engined double-deckers were twelve Daimler Fleetlines in 1965, and were followed in 1967 by eleven more and twelve Leyland Atlanteans. Twelve more Fleetlines arrived in 1971. Numbered 1-34, all were bodied by Alexander. The bodies were built to an 'intermediate' overall height, resulting in both types looking much the same – a Fleetline would normally have been less high but the Atlanteans were the PDR1/2 model. In this 1967 view in Dewsbury Bus Station, brand new 22 is working local service G and behind is number 16 on the 1A to Leeds. These rear-engined vehicles would introduce one-person double-decker operation in due course. *Geoffrey Morant*

A severe vehicle shortage In 1968/69 resulted in vehicles being acquired from several fellow THC / NBC companies. Perhaps the most surprising were the elderly ECW-bodied Bristol Ks – five from United Automobile Services in Darlington and six from Keighley-West Yorkshire and York-West Yorkshire, the latter at first on hire. This is 169, one of those from United, loading in Dewsbury with a Bradford Leyland PD3 in the background. The Bristols ran for a year. *Nicholas Harris*

The seven vehicles from South Wales Transport in 1969 had some mechanical commonality with the Regent Vs. Numbered 156-163 they were AEC-Park Royal Bridgemasters new in 1960/61. In this May 1969 view, taken soon after its arrival, 156 is still in South Wales' unrelieved dark red livery. They, too, were withdrawn after just over a year. *Nicholas Harris*

The Independents

Baddeley Brothers, Farsley Omnibus, Kippax Motors, Ford of Ackworth, Ezra Layock, J J Longstaff, Pennine, United Services, South Yorkshire, J Wood & Sons

In spite of the ambitions of the railways and the BET and Tilling groups in the late 1920s and the 1930s, the area was one where independent operators resisted that threat and survived beyond the formation of the PTE and, in many cases, deregulation. The two largest, West Riding and Bullock and Sons, have their own section of this book but any picture of the area would not be complete without the others that survived into the 1970s. Their background was as interesting and varied as their fleets. Starting in 1905 Ezra Layock was one of the first bus operators in Yorkshire and indeed the country; its 'heavyweight' fleet reflected that history. Neighbour Pennine's splendid orange, grey and black fleet was also heavy – mainly Leylands including notable ex Show models. Surrounded by West Yorkshire and Ribble, the firm developed a close relationship with Ribble. J J Longstaff and neighbour Joseph Wood ran a service right in the middle of Yorkshire Woollen's territory and Woollen eventually had to coordinate its own service with theirs. Across the other side of the area, three operators, each with their own fleet but with a common livery and appropriate fleet name of United Services, shared services and thereby maintained their independence. The mighty coach operator Wallace Arnold also had a short involvement in bus operation when it bought Farsley Omnibus and Kippax & District. South Yorkshire Motors' immaculate blue buses were the result of a Bullock family dispute. These tough and proud firms were as much a part of the area's transport as any of the larger municipal or group operators.

Baddeley Bros, Holmfirth

In 1930 Leonard and Jesse Baddeley had pioneered a service from Huddersfield to Sheffield via Honley, Stocksbridge and Deepcar. Falling foul of the Traffic Commissioners, they eventually settled for a truncated route to Deepcar where a connection was made with a Sheffield Corporation service for on-going travel. Photographed outside Holmfirth post office in June 1967 Baddeley's number 87, a Weymann-bodied Albion Nimbus formerly with Halifax JOC, has just left the departure stand in the bus station. Ten of these vehicles had been in the Halifax fleet and in 1967 Baddeley's manager, John Steel, purchased two of them initially for transporting workers to the construction site of the M62 motorway at Scammonden. *Omnibus Society/Peter Henson*

This Bedford SB with Mulliner bodywork (it had no fleet number) was new in 1962 as a workmen's bus for the United Steel Companies of Rotherham and passed to the Primrose Valley coach company at Filey before being acquired by Baddeley in 1962. Unique in the Baddeley fleet, this Bedford/ Mulliner combination was much used by the armed forces. Pictured at the Penistone stand in the Holmfirth bus station the background will be familiar to those many viewers of the BBC 'Last of the Summer Wine' series. The destination Dunford Bridge suggests that a short working on the hourly service to Penistone (Cubley) is about to be operated. Alternate buses ran over this sparsely populated bleak Pennine route via Dunford Bridge or Victoria, Millhouse and Thurlstone. *Roy Marshall*

Fleet number 105 was one of a pair of fourth-hand Yeates-bodied Bedford SBs operated by Baddeley in the early seventies. The vehicle window pillars indicate the Pegasus model and the Bedford chassis was modified by Yeates to accommodate a body with an entrance forward of the front axle. Fitted with coach seats and classified as dual purpose this useful vehicle was used as a one person operated service bus as well as for private hire and contract work. New to R Store of Stainforth, it arrived at Holmfirth via Yorkshire Traction who in turn had acquired it with the business of Mexborough and Swinton. It is pictured here in the Hollowgate garage yard; several buses were swamped here in the infamous Holmfirth Flood on Whit Monday 1944. *Nicholas Harris*

Farsley Omnibus Co and Kippax Motors (Wallace Arnold group)

Based in Richardshaw Lane, Stanningley, the long established Farsley Omnibus Company operated a service from Pudsey to Horsforth. Somewhat surprisingly in 1952 it was bought by the Wallace Arnold group, then the country's largest coach operator with a fleet of over 200 coaches but no buses. In 1956/57 eight of the group's 1949 Wilks & Meade-bodied Daimler CVD6 coaches were rebodied with new Roe double-deck bodies for use by its bus subsidiaries – Farsley, Kippax, and Hardwick's at Scarborough. This picture shows MUB 433 in Pudsey bus station in February 1968. *Roy Marshall*

The Wallace Arnold group added two Leyland PD3s with Roe bodywork, one in 1963 and this one, HNW 366D, in 1966. It is pictured at the Pudsey terminus in February 1968 along with a Yorkshire Woollen AEC Regent V. Together with fellow Wallace Arnold subsidiary Kippax Motors, Farsley Omnibus was sold to Leeds City Transport in March 1968, although no vehicles passed to Leeds. *Roy Marshall*

Originally named Yellow Bus service when it started in 1924, Kippax & District ran a service from Leeds through Garforth to Ledston Luck Colliery to the east of Leeds. In 1948 two new Leyland-bodied PD2s, GWX 823/24, joined the fleet of half a dozen buses. The business was purchased by Wallace Arnold in 1956 and the name changed to Kippax Motors. The second of the pair is pictured in Leeds Central Bus Station Leeds on 9th May 1959 ready for a short working to Garforth. *John Kaye*

In addition to an ex-Ribble PD1, Kippax received three of the former Wallace Arnold Daimler CVD6 / Wilks & Meade coaches rebodied in 1957 by Roe as double deckers. LNW 869 came straight to Kippax and the vehicle shown in this picture, MUM 461, first ran for Farsley and was transferred to Kippax in 1958. The picture was taken outside Ledston Luck colliery in June 1962. *Travelens/Vic Nutton*

Ford, Ackworth

New to Ribble in 1948 Burlingham-bodied Leyland PD1 BRN 282 was one of the first thirty 'White Lady' double-deck coaches. Sold in 1959 it was bought by John Turton of Ackworth and, along with his business and service from Pontefract to Ackworth passed to Ford in September 1962. In May 1964 Ford moved from Fairburn to the former Turton premises in Bell Lane, Ackworth. Behind in this May 1963 picture of it in Pontefract bus station is West Riding AEC Regent III DHL 928. *Roy Marshall*

Pictured in Pontefract Bus Station in March 1972 is CYG 432H a Leyland Leopard with Willowbrook bodywork, which Ford purchased new. The former West Yorkshire Road Car Co Bristol Lodekka OWX 161 alongside is owned by H Wray & Sons ('Ideal') of Hoyle Mill, near Barnsley. *Roy Marshall*

Ford's fleet of around half a dozen buses and coaches also included these two bus-bodied Bedford VALs. Pictured in Pontefract bus station in September 1968 Willowbrook-bodied 351 GYG was awaitng departure time for Ackworth. Ford bought it new in 1964. *Alan Mortimer*

Also in Pontefract bus station in September 1968 was Duple Midland-bodied 4230 PE, which Ford acquired in October 1965 from a dealer who had in turn bought it from Richmond, Epsom. In addition to the Pontefract to Ackworth service. Ford operated several colliery and schools services. *Alan Mortimer*

Ezra Layock, Barnoldswick

Commencing in 1905, Ezra Layock Ltd was one of the first bus operators in the country only becoming a limited company in 1952. Laycock was based in Barnoldswick just inside the Yorkshire border but were originally in Cowling. In addition to local services in Barnoldswick and Skipton, it operated important stage services from Barnoldswick to Skipton and Skipton to Carleton. The fleet was some 6 buses and 4 coaches. In March 1959 Ezra Laycock purchased this Park Royal-style Roe-bodied AEC Reliance fleet number 53, seen here in November 1969 turning into Skipton bus station on the long established service from Barnoldswick, acquired with take over of Premier in 1928. *Geoffrey Morant*

Above This AEC Regal III with Plaxton Highway body, new in 1959 was acquired by Laycock from Rhind of Wakefield in 1962. Numbered 66 it is pictured leaving Skipton bus station in April 1967 on the service to Carleton acquired with the business of J T Hey (Silver Star) in August 1961. *Geoffrey Morant*

Below Silver Star's livery was red and grey, as shown in this 1960 picture of Duple-bodied Bedford OB GOU 721 in Skipton bus station with Laycock's AEC-Park Royal Monocoach 51 behind, loading on the Barnoldswick stand. *Peter Roberts*

It was 1964 before Ezra Laycock acquired more double-deckers since its original one in 1906. These were Leylands from Southdown and Ribble plus two Northern Counties- bodied AEC Regent IIIs from Western SMT. They were mainly used on school and works contracts but BCS 453 is seen here on the stage service in Skipton in September 1965 only a few days after it joined the Laycock fleet. In the background is Keighley-West Yorkshire Bristol Lodekka KDX 144. *Roy Marshall*

Two Willowbrook-bodied AEC Regal IIIs, new to Trent in 1950, were bought in November 1961 to replace the ex-Silver Star Bedford OBs. Numbered 64/65 they remained in the fleet for less than twelve months. The second of the two is shown here in Skipton bus station on a snowy day, appropriately working the former Silver Star service. Laycock's fleet was numbered in a single series, although this was slightly inconsistent in that some vehicles had no fleet number. *Geoffrey Morant*

Passing Bell Vue Mills (home of Sylko sewing cotton) on Broughton Road, Skipton is XHW 408 an ECW-bodied Bristol LS5G on the service from Barnoldswick. The picture was taken just before the Laycock business was sold to Pennine Motor Services in August 1972, Pennine retaining the Laycock garage in Barnoldswick. *Omnibus Society/Peter Henson*

149

Longstaff, Mirfield

J J Longstaff of Mirfield operated a single but important service between Dewsbury and Mirfield via Knowl. Right in the middle of Yorkshire Woollen's territory it was coordinated with the similar services of Wood of Mirfield and Yorkshire Woollen's own service. The early withdrawal of London Transport Cravens-bodied RTs gave provincial operators the opportunity to upgrade their fleets. Longstaff acquired KGK 759 in January 1958 from Scott's Greys of Darlington; this picture was taken soon after it arrived. It ran until 1963 when it was replaced by a later, Park Royal-bodied RT. *Geoffrey Morant*

In October 1968 Plaxton-bodied Albion Aberdonian XUP 507 passes Dewsbury Bus Station en route to Mirfield. Longstaff acquired the bus from County Durham operator Armstrong of Ebchester in January 1967; it would spend four years in the fleet. *Geoffrey Morant*

Originally new to Garelochhead Coach Services, Northern Counties-bodied Daimler CSG6-30 passed to Cunningham's Bus Services of Paisley before purchase by Longstaff in November 1967. Although the Mirfield service was coordinated with Yorkshire Woollen District and Woods of Mirfield, it was not joint and Yorkshire Woollen's service terminated in Dewsbury bus station whereas Wood and Longstaff stopped in Longcauseway, across from the bus station, later moving to Rishworth Road where this picture was taken in October 1971. *Nicholas Harris*

RYG 999L was Longstaff's first new double-decker. A Daimler Fleetline CRL6 fitted with Roe bodywork to Park Royal's standard design of the time, it arrived in September 1972, replacing Daimler LSN 286. March 1975, *Roy Marshall*

151

Pennine, Gargrave

Commencing business in the 1920s and owned by the Simpson family, Pennine Motor Services Ltd, of Gargrave, near Skipton, was (and still is at the time of writing) an important operator, for years its fleet of around 15 was Leylands, most bought new. GWT 317/18 were Burlingham-bodied PS1s new in 1947. Here GWT 317 is about to depart Skipton Bus Station for Gargrave; it ran with Pennine until 1961 but, as was the case with the Pennine fleet, was in fine condition when photographed in 1960. *Peter Roberts*

Pennine acquired two significant Leyland motor show models. The first, bought in November 1951 was MTC 757- a Leyland Royal Tiger with Brush bodywork. New the previous year, it had been used by Leyland to demonstrate the then new Royal Tiger to large companies and municipal operators. Its task completed, it joined the Pennine fleet in November 1951 and ran for sixteen years. May 1963. *Roy Marshall*

Like MTC 757 this Royal Tiger was exhibited at the Commercial Motor Show in 1950 and was then demonstrated to numerous operators before joining the Pennine fleet in September 1952. It had the prototype of Leyland's own coach body, later supplied (in slightly modified form) in quantity to Ribble and other BET fleets. Withdrawn in February 1970 it was retained by Pennine for possible future restoration, and at the time of writing, was still owned by the company. It was used on stage services as in this picture, taken in August 1960. *Peter Roberts*

Pennine had a close working relationship with Ribble and its principal stage services, Skipton – Settle – Lancaster – Morecambe; Skipton – Gargrave – Malham, were joint with Ribble. When Ribble sold its Leyland bodied Royal Tigers, one of the best is said to have been picked out for Pennine. ECK 610 joined the fleet in January 1963 – Pennine had bought one of its own, new in 1953. When Ribble closed its Skipton garage it was purchased by Pennine and, many years later, became Pennine's head office. *Peter Roberts*

Two more Royal Tigers followed in 1954, this time with Roe bodies. NWT 329 and NWT 807 and would serve in the Pennine fleet for twenty years. In this picture taken by Geoffrey Morant in November 1969, crew-operated NWT 329 is leaving Skipton on the Settle service.
Geoffrey Morant

After another Leyland demonstrator – this time a Comet coach – three new Duple-bodied Leyland Tiger Cubs joined the fleet. Two were coaches but the first, UWX 277, had a Duple (Midland) Donington body with bus seats. New in May 1958, it was principally used on the long service from Skipton to Lancaster, jointly operated with Ribble. This picture shows it in Lancaster bus station in June 1966. *Geoffrey Morant*

With the limestone outcrop of Giggleswick Scar in the background Roe-bodied Leyland Leopard 240 CWY, new in May 1963, had just completed the steep climb of Buckhaw Brow out of Giggleswick on what was then the A65 trunk road, en route from Skipton to Ingleton in August 1967. It ran for thirteen years in the Pennine fleet before passing to Tillingbourne Bus Company Ltd of Surrey. *Alan Mortimer*

Pennine bought more Leopards, most were 49-seat 36ft-long but UWU 521F was a 30ft PSU4 with a 41-seat Willowbrook bus body with coach seats. It was new in April 1968 but its lower seating capacity made it less useful and it was sold in July 1970. In this November 1969 picture it is arriving at Skipton from Lancaster. *Geoffrey Morant*

South Yorkshire, Pontefract

The Bullock brothers formed B&S Motors in 1913. Friction between the brothers came to a head through a High Court case in 1928 whereupon Ernest, the eldest, left and with his son, Reg, purchased the ailing South Yorkshire MotorCompany, basing it in the former B&S garage in Cornmarket, Pontefract. Established and new services were developed radiating from Pontefract, including Leeds, Barnsley, Doncaster and Selby. The bus fleet, plus a few coaches, mainly Albions and then Leylands, seldom exceeded 20 and was always very well turned out and with above average seating. The major part of the business, however, was three Main Ford car dealerships in the area. South Yorkshire was one of the first companies in the area to buy the Leyland Atlantean – two arrived in 1963 followed by further Atlanteans, Daimler Fleetlines and Leyland Olympians. Reg Bullock, the long serving Managing Director died in 1968 and his nephew John McCloy, a grandson of Ernest, took the helm. The Ford dealerships were sold and the company reconstituted as South Yorkshire Road Transport, introducing more coaches and a short-lived express service between Hull and Manchester. It was sold to the Caldaire Group in 1994, later becoming part of Arriva.

After the fleet's first four double-deckers – utility Daimler CWA6s new in 1944, of which Brush-bodied 53 is shown here – South Yorkshire returned to Albion. New in 1950 and mainstay of the fleet at the time, Strachan-bodied Albion CX37 72 was one of four similar buses. Pontefract Bus Station is the setting for both pictures, showing the heavy body refurbishment they were given later in their service life. May 1962, *Geoff Lumb,* May 1963. *Roy Marshall*

With Albion ceasing production of double-deck chassis, South Yorkshire turned to Leyland. 76 was one of four Leyland-bodied PD2/12 purchased in 1950. Numbered 73-76 they were used on the longer routes, such as Leeds to Doncaster. Most had a service life of 20 years. *Roy Marshall*

The choice of bodywork for the next two double-deckers was unusual. Long-established commercial vehicle body maker S H Bond of Manchester made a short-lived entry into bus bodywork, producing only about forty bus bodies. New in 1954, numbers 77/78 were Leyland PD2/20 with Bond lowbridge bodies. The setting for this June 1968 view is a Selby Market Day when Park Street replaced the Market Place bus terminus. Employees referred to number 77 as 'sunset strip' after the television series of the time. The two were the first South Yorkshire buses with platform doors and concealed radiators. *Geoffrey Morant*

Numbers 79 and 80 were Leyland PD2/20 with Park Royal lowbridge bodies with South Yorkshire's usual high standard interior with fluorescent interior lighting and high backed seats. This picture shows number 79 in the bus station of South Yorkshire's home town of Pontefract along with a former Southend Corporation Leyland PD2 HJN 841 running for Ideal Service and West Riding 134 – a Cummins-engined Daimler Roadliner. *Nicholas Harris*

This Albion CX13 was new in 1950 as Burlingham-bodied single-deck coach number 57. In 1958 its body was moved onto one of South Yorkshire's earlier Albion chassis and in 1958 57's chassis was overhauled and modified to CX37 specification. It was then rebodied as a double-decker by Roe and renumbered 81. It also received a new registration number – something that happened fairly often in the area. *Travelens/Vic Nutton*

Two Leyland PD3s with Roe lowbridge bodies followed in 1960. In this September 1973 picture, number 82 has just left Leeds Central Bus Station for Pontefract. *Geoffrey Morant*

South Yorkshire was quick to adopt the Leyland Atlantean, with two each in 1963 and 1965 with Weymann bodies. To achieve the low height required for some of South Yorkshire's routes, they had the awkward 'lowbridge' arrangement, whereby the last two rows of seats in the upper deck had the side gangway arrangement of lowbridge bodies on front-engined chassis. The passengers can be seen squeezed up against the rear offside upper-deck windows in this picture of the fourth, number 87, leaving Doncaster bus station. *Nicholas Harris*

They were followed in 1967 by numbers 88 and 89, which had the PDR1/2 chassis that had a lower height than the previous model. The attractively styled body was by Roe. Continuing the style of the PDs, all the Atlanteans had a lower seating capacity than average (70) and semi-luxury seats. This picture shows brand new 88 loading in Leeds Central Bus Station for Doncaster on 26th August 1967. *Don Akrigg*

Still with only 70 seats, two Leyland AN68 Atlanteans (90/91) arrived in 1971. They had Northern Counties bodies and this body builder was to provide bodywork for Daimler Fleetlines and Olympians obtained over the next few years. Fleet number 91 leaves Doncaster's North Bus Station in June 71. *Geoffrey Morant*

There was something of a change when this updated and striking new livery was introduced in 1973, possibly prompted by the coming formation of the South Yorkshire PTE, which would use the words South Yorkshire in its fleetname. This is Fleetline 94 in Pontefract Bus Station in 1974 with repainted PD2 number 80 parked behind. *Roy Marshall*

United Services

United Services was an operating name for three firms – Phyllis Bingley trading as W R & P Bingley of Kinsley (fleet of some 12 buses and coaches), Cooper Brothers of South Kirby (around 3 to 5 buses) and W Everett & Son of South Kirby (some 5 buses and 8 coaches). The three shared operation of services from Wakefield to Doncaster via Kinsley and South Kirby, and Wakefield to Hemsworth via Kinsley. Each had its own fleet but the vehicles used for United Services were all finished in the same blue livery, although Phyllis Bingley also had a substantial coach fleet of her own plus a single Bedford SB bus, finished in red and cream. Everett sold to Bingley in 1969 and Cooper followed suit in 1977.

The only double-deck vehicles purchased new by any of the United Services members were two Roe-bodied Regent Vs, UWT 875/76 bought by Phyllis Bingley in 1957 and for many years were her principal contribution to the service. In this 1963 picture, the second of them waits at Doncaster's Marshgate bus station, the southern terminus of the route from Wakefield. The conductress carries her Bellgraphic ticket machine – each of the three constituent operators used a different ticket system.
Richard Simons

In 1960 Bingley bought two former Ribble 'White Lady' Burlingham-bodied Leyland PD1 coaches, replacing them after some two years with two of the later East Lancs-bodied PD2 'White Ladies'. Formerly Ribble 1242/50, DCK 213/21 still had their coach seating and gave an above average ride between Wakefield and Doncaster. This picture of DCK 213 was taken shortly after that above. *Richard Simons*

After the war, Bingley had three new Daimler CVD6 – two single-deck buses and a coach – and an underfloor-engined Daimler Freeline coach, also new, to which was added this Duple-bodied Daimler CVD6 double-decker in 1954. New in 1948 to Skill, Nottingham it was Bingley's last Daimler. Roy Marshall took this picture of LTO 10 in May 1963. *Roy Marshall*

Bingley's local service from South Kirkby (Saxon Mount) to Frickley (Broad Lane) was not part of the United Services arrangement and was worked with a vehicle from Bingley's own red and cream fleet. For a time the fleet included a former RAF Bedford SB bus but the service was more usually worked with a coach, although one of Bingley's blue United Services buses would sometimes be used. Here in May 1969 it is being worked by Plaxton-bodied Bedford SB PHL 271. *Roy Marshall*

In April 1969 Everett acquired this former Aldershot & District East Lancs-bodied Dennis Loline and it was a positive move away from the unpopular side gangway of the lowbridge double deckers. It was, however, the last double-decker to enter the fleets. The extra capacity of the 30ft-long Loline was also welcome, as seen in this picture of it in October 1969 leaving Wakefield with a full load of seated and standing passengers, a month before the Everett business was sold to Bingley – the sale including SOU 473. *Geoffrey Morant*

Everett had a mixed fleet including several former Ribble Leylands similar to those operated by the other two partners. Acquired in 1968 and photographed a month before the business passed to Phyllis Bingley, this Duple-bodied Guy Arab had started life with Red & White Services of Chepstow. *Geoffrey Morant*

The smallest of the three operators was Cooper Brothers whose first double-decker was acquired locally – from Doncaster Corporation in 1960. Only seven years old, MDT 220 was an AEC Regent III with a Roe low bridge body, Doncaster having decided to dispose of its lowbridge double-deckers. It is pictured leaving Wakefield for Hemsworth on the same day as the Loline above – but with not such a good load. *Geoffrey Morant*

Former Ribble buses were always a good buy and Cooper Brothers bought three – two PD2s and a PD1, and this is the first. Acquired in September 1960 CCK 646 was a Brush-bodied PD2. New in 1949 and pictured here in 1962, it remained in the fleet for six years. Two identifying features of the Cooper Bros fleet were the twin spotlights and the CB in the centre of the fleetname. *John May*

Hunched over the steering wheel as he waits for departure in Wakefield bus station in September 1968, the cloth-capped driver of Bingley's new Willowbrook-bodied AEC Swift glares at the photographer. The uniformed conductress stands at the front of the saloon for the bus was two-person operated. However, with one-person operation in mind, Bingley and Cooper Brothers both turned to single-deckers – new heavyweight chassis in Bingley's case. *Alan Mortimer*

Pictured in June 1971 leaving Doncaster's North Bus Station for Wakefield is AWX 118G, a Plaxton-bodied Leyland Leopard purchased new by Bingley in 1969. Further vehicles of this type and 'bus grant' coaches equipped for service work resulted in the withdrawal of the remaining double-deck vehicles. *Geoffrey Morant*

In contrast to Bingley, Cooper Brothers turned to lightweight Bedfords for its new single deckers. New in 1971 OWT 549K was a Willowbrook-bodied Bedford VAM pictured in Wakefield with a light load for Doncaster. *Roy Marshall*

An exception to the lightweight Bedford single-deckers bought by Cooper Brothers was this Leyland Panther Cub with Park Royal bodywork. New to Manchester Corporation, which became part of the SELNEC PTE in 1969, it joined the Cooper fleet from SELNEC. SELNEC sold the Manchester Panther Cubs in 1971/72 and Cooper bought ANF 161B which had been fitted with the larger O.600 engine by the Corporation. It joined the Bingley fleet when the Cooper business was sold to Bingley in 1977. It was new to the fleet when this picture was taken in April 1972. *John Kaye*

J Wood & Sons

Joseph Wood & Sons Ltd of Mirfield operated the Dewsbury – Mirfield service, coordinated with Longstaff and Yorkshire Woollen. The smartly finished fleet was three or four buses and half a dozen coaches, several of which were Crossleys. Its first double-decker was one of the more notable vehicles in the area. New to Baxter of Airdrie in June 1949 Crossley DD42/7 EVD 406 had lowbridge bodywork by Scottish Commercial and arrived with Wood in August 1953. The body failed its first ministry test with Wood and EVD 406 was rebodied with a Roe highbridge body in April 1955, after which it spent a further 12 years on the joint service between Dewsbury and Mirfield. Withdrawn in 1967, Woods kept it and it was carefully restored by Joseph Wood's son, Colin. This picture shows it at the Dewsbury terminus in Long Causeway on a wet April day in 1963. *Roy Marshall*

Originally new to Kitchin of Pudsey, this Burlingham-bodied Atkinson PL745H came to Wood from Samuel Ledgard, which had acquired it when it took over Kitchin's stage carriage routes in April 1957. In this view taken on Longcauseway Dewsbury NWW 805 is operating a short working to Savile Arms duplicating the Crossley behind which would work the full route to Ings Grove Park, Mirfield. *Peter Roberts*

167

To replace the Crossley, in November 1967 Wood purchased this former Leyland Atlantean demonstrator with Park Royal bodywork. It had spent almost three years on demonstration duties and would give another thirteen years service for Wood's. This April 1975 picture of fleet number 30 was taken at the Rishworth Road terminus in Dewsbury. *Roy Marshall*

The advent of the bus grant saw Wood's purchase this Leyland Leopard with dual-purpose Plaxton bodywork. In this view the vehicle has just pulled way from the Rishworth Road terminus in Dewsbury. Wood's also had a small coach fleet and FWR 232J's coach seating made the vehicle ideal for contract and private hire work when required. *John Kaye*